THE FIFTH SPARROW

An autobiography

THE FIFTH SPARROW

An autobiography

M. L. SKINNER

With a foreword by
MARY DURACK

ANGUS AND ROBERTSON

First published in the United Kingdom in 1973 by
ANGUS AND ROBERTSON (U.K.) LTD
2 Fisher Street, London
102 Glover Street, Cremorne, Sydney
107 Elizabeth Street, Melbourne
89 Anson Road, Singapore

ISBN 0 207 12569 4

Printed in Australia at The Griffin Press, Adelaide

CONTENTS

LIST OF PLATES

between pages 76 and 77

The author, about the time of her meeting with D. H. Lawrence in 1922

The author, seventy years of age, at the time of writing *The Fifth Sparrow*

Birthplace of Mollie Skinner—the Officers Quarters, St. George's Terrace, Perth

Sir John and Lady Winthrop Hackett c. 1900 when they first met the author

Colonel and Mrs James Skinner and five of their seven children, Ireland 1882

D. H. Lawrence's letter of 15 November 1923 to Mollie Skinner

Jacket of the American edition of *The Boy in the Bush*

South-west district hospital of which the author was matron in 1923

Group Settlement in the south-west in 1923—a scheme 'too hastily and optimistically devised'

A page from Mollie Skinner's unpublished novel *Eve in the Land of Nod*

A letter to Mary Durack from Mollie Skinner, 21 October 1939

FOREWORD

by ✑Mary Durack

It seemed unlikely, to say the least, that the author of *Lady Chatterley's Lover* should have become associated in a literary way with a middle-aged Quaker spinster of fairly Victorian standards. The situation, however, was not as incongruous as it may sound, for the unusual aspects of Mollie Skinner's personality endure far beyond her grave.

In appearance she had the chunky, interesting quality of hand-thrown pottery and her mind the fascination of an antique collection in which one discovered with delight unexpected treasures among a conglomeration of serviceable items and irrelevant bric-a-brac.

By the time of her meeting with Lawrence, Mollie had led a full, useful and unusual life. She was born in Perth in 1876, her father the English Captain of the Royal Irish Regiment and her mother a member of one of Western Australia's prominent early families. When she was about two, Captain Skinner and his family returned to England with the last Imperial troops to serve in the forty-nine year-old colony. Mollie's childhood was spent in England, Ireland and Scotland in circumstances she has described in this book. Her education was hampered by poor sight and during her teens she spent much time, under painful treatment, in a darkened room. The condition improved, but her sight was never normal and the threat of blindness hung over her at all times. For this disability, however, she was compensated by a keen and perceptive intelligence and a spirit of unusual courage and independence that led her, against all the conventions of her age and class, to complete her nursing training before returning to Australia in 1900. While still in England she wrote sketches for the London *Daily Mail* and when back in Perth became a social writer on the *Morning Herald*.

After some years, during which time she gained considerable experience as a nurse in country districts, she went back to England and trained for her midwifery certificate in the slums of London. She thereafter returned to Australia, produced a textbook on midwifery, went into partnership in a city hospital, sold out and took herself off once more to nurse in London.

At the outbreak of World War I she joined Lady Minto's Nursing Service and served in India and Burma until 1916, after which she served until the end of the war with Queen Alexandra's Military Nursing Service and the Australian Medical Service. During this time she wrote *Letters of a V.A.D.*, which was published under the *nom de plume* of R. E. Leake.

Back in Western Australia, she became matron of hospitals in the newly opened Group Settlement districts and thereafter, in partnership with her Quaker friend Miss Ellen Beakbane, she ran a guest house named *Leithdale* in the charming hills resort of Darlington, near Perth. It was during this period that she met D. H. Lawrence who, with his wife Frieda, was a guest in her establishment.

I can well understand why Lawrence should, as she tells us, have continually escaped the fashionable house guests to seek her out in the laundry. He had been given a copy of her *Letters of a V.A.D.*, which had evidently impressed him with its vitality, freshness and originality. 'You have been given the divine spark,' he chided her, 'and you would bury it in a napkin!'

It was Lawrence who inspired her to embark on the writing of a novel that was later to appear under their joint names as *The Boy in the Bush*. The success of this combined effort was never to be repeated, but Lawrence had been right about Mollie. She did have the 'spark', as anyone who knew her must have realised. Her mind was intensely, restlessly creative, not only in a literary but an everyday sense. She gave of its vitality not only in the best of her writing, but in all her human relationships, in her gift for communication which transcended all barriers of class, creed, politics and generation, the encouragement she gave to struggling writers and the real pleasure she took in any success they might achieve.

I don't remember having met Mollie at any particular time. She seems always to have been somewhere around in my life, at first appearing at odd times in the homes of relatives and mutual friends. Our closer association began in 1938 with the formation of the Western Australian branch of the Fellowship of Australian Writers, of which we were both foundation members. Cost her what it may, travelling from the hills in all weathers, mostly by bus, Mollie never missed a meeting. Her especial contribution to the Executive Committee was a mixture of commonsense judgement and impractical whimsy, a tolerance of political differences and a remarkable talent for cutting red tape. When confronted with a problem she would supply not one, but several, alternative solutions, some inspired, others hilariously inapplicable. She never pretended to great erudition; often she would say: 'I'm not at all educated, you know—but if you want my opinion. . . .' She would give it in any case. She was made an Honorary Life Member of the Fellowship at about the same time as Katherine Susannah Prichard and Walter Murdoch.

Mollie belonged to a time when many women of intellectual leanings were much drawn to the occult. She herself was fascinated by mysticism and the supernatural and revelled in discussions with people of strong religious convictions. It is not hard to understand, therefore, that when under the influence of Sybil Dauney in London she was an ardent Anglo-Catholic, that on her return to Australia she veered towards the Theosophism of her friend Muriel Chase, and that she later still espoused the Quaker faith of her business associate Nellie Beakbane. She was a strong believer in mystical 'voices' and the invisible, gently directing 'hand on the shoulder' for defiance of which one would in some way be held answerable. In fact, when she first spoke to me of her autobiography she intended calling it *The Hand on My Shoulder*.

Although no proselytiser, she wielded a considerable influence, particularly on young people in their moments of doubt, indecision or failing confidence. As one of her young friends replied when asked why she was giving up a well-paid teaching job to help out at a poverty-stricken mission in North Kimberley: 'I have an uncanny suspicion it's Mollie Skinner's "hand".'

Of the many people of all walks of life who visited her in the little hills cottage she inherited from her mother, there was never one who did not come away refreshed in spirit even if, since conversations with Mollie were apt to fly off at tangents, they had not got to the point they came to discuss.

Any small sum of money she was able to accumulate she never kept for herself. 'A gay lad,' she used to say, 'need carry no more than his horn of water.' And that was the spirit in which she lived, happy if there was enough in her purse to see her from day to day, and with a sort of gaiety, almost of insouciance, about her. She always appeared unharassed, unhurried, as though she had all the time in the world, but in fact she worked hard at her writing, at her considerable correspondence and at the important business of being a friend. She never neglected to carry out the good intentions that can so easily be set aside for 'another time'. Where I was concerned this meant visits, with appropriate little gifts, to inspect new babies and the immediate writing of encouraging letters about the appearance in print of literary efforts, however small.

Typical both of this heart-warming response and of her conviction that one must, at all costs, fulfil one's destiny is a note written soon after the birth of my first child in 1939. It would seem to have been inspired by a letter to the paper commenting on a story I had written about that time:

> Sunday 21-10-39
> Darlington
>
> I can't help writing to you about the letter in yesterday's 'West' . . . re your story. What I want to convey is a peculiar sort of congratulation, that you have touched the heart of your readers. If you have that gift—*as* you have that gift nothing must stop you! not marriage, or Patsy or war or anything. And it won't for you have marriage and Patsy and war and everything—all in one year . . .

Mollie would have been shocked at the suggestion that anyone should shirk responsibility, but she was, ahead of her time, an advocate of 'women's lib' in her constant assertion that women no less than men, should use to its fullest extent any talent given them.

It was Guy Howarth, when reader in English literature at the Sydney University, who first suggested that she should write her autobiography, giving an account of her own formative years and describing the stage she had reached at the time of her now historic encounter with D. H. Lawrence.

Then in her seventies and with rapidly failing eyesight, Mollie was hesitant to embark on such an undertaking. What finally decided her was the appearance of several post-mortem biographical accounts of Lawrence highlighting, as she thought, the less attractive aspects of his character.

'I would like to tell people,' she said, 'that he was not the horrible person his critics make him out to have been . . . He revealed himself to me as a man of great spiritual integrity who had not discarded the long, long thoughts of boyhood . . . He was not a sensual man but a creature of fire.'

So, with the encouragement and practical help of Mrs Marjorie

Rees, then Honorary Secretary of the Fellowship of Writers (W.A. Branch), indefatigable typist and adviser to most of its members, including myself, Mollie set to work.

The book was shaping well, Mollie posting off her ms. chapter by chapter to be transformed from her own hit-and-miss typing into clear script, when quite suddenly she went completely blind. This calamity she accepted with characteristic courage and dignified independence. She had been faced with blindness all her life and it was not going to defeat her now. Her main concern was her unfinished autobiography. Marjorie Rees, realising that without this interest her future would be bleak indeed, urged her to continue and this she did, typing fumblingly and calling upon Quaker neighbours to read back to her.

When the stage for rewriting was achieved Marjorie suggested that Mollie come to stay with her. In a talk for the Fellowship delivered after Mollie's death and later published in *Westerly*, Marjorie described the forebodings with which she made this approach:

> The whole situation was difficult . . . Could Mollie endure our tiny home; my haphazard housekeeping, my garlic and olive oil cooking messes; and above all, our atomic child, Tony? Could I type, cook, be a gracious hostess, cope with the daily: 'Have I got a clean shirt, dear?' from my husband, battle with Tony and not become irritable and nasty?
>
> I needn't have worried. Mollie's warmth, friendliness and patience smoothed out everything. Tony behaved angelically and they became great friends.
>
> Between us—my reading aloud to Mollie for corrections—also difficult as she was then very deaf—we knocked the book into some sort of shape. It ended with Mollie's meeting with Lawrence. At that time she thought this was enough, but later, after she had left our home to stay with relatives, she decided to include her association with him up to the time of his death, and her own life during that period.
>
> Then came another set-back. She became seriously ill and a major operation was necessary. She nearly died and I am sure would never have recovered but for her determination to finish the book. In practically no time she was back at her typewriter. The blackout of her blindness lightened a little and at times she could see, very foggily, for short intervals. That was enough for her to carry on. She finished the autobiography and wrote newspaper articles, short stories and several talks for the A.B.C.,

and continued writing till the end of her life in 1955. In fact, I received the manuscript of a radio talk in the post about half an hour before I heard the news of her death. This talk was subsequently broadcast by Catherine King in the A.B.C. Women's Session.

It is clear that but for Marjorie's selfless and devoted help this autobiography would have remained one of the sundry unfinished projects—including a life of John Forrest—that Mollie had at some time assayed. Her executors put the ms. of *The Fifth Sparrow* into the hands of the Fellowship of Writers, and Henrietta Drake-Brockman, during her presidency, tried to launch it through various channels. When I inherited the problem the reason for its rejection at last became clear to me. Just as Mollie's myopia had caused her to see objects impressionistically, rather than in detail, so she had seen life, often indeed getting nearer the truth than had she been preoccupied by precise documentation. Lawrence had told her to write from the heart, to write about what she knew and let what she didn't go hang. 'Construction? You need none,' he had told her . . . 'You spoil things by rewriting . . . When you've done 80,000 words, throw down your pen.'

This advice, whatever its worth as concerns the writing of fiction, led only to confusion when applied to the historical background of an autobiography. Mollie had not, at the best of times, been much worried by such details as dates and sequence. Unable to correct her own material and too deaf properly to hear it read back, she had produced a manuscript that was like a garden choked with weeds.

It was to Marjorie Rees, who had given as much direction as was possible during the writing of the book, that I went for help and advice on the necessary editing and with whom I worked in checking facts and sequence and deleting repetitious material. The result is the book in its present form, which we feel is as Mollie, given time and sight, would have wished it presented.

The original, unchecked and unabridged ms., together with the working copy used in the editing process, are to be found in the Battye Library, Perth, Western Australia.

Both Marjorie and I would like to express our gratitude to the staffs of the Battye Library and West Australian Newspapers, and to Mollie Skinner's relatives, especially her sister Mrs Dollie Law, for help in the completion of this project and in the obtaining of photographs. Our warm thanks are also due to Professor Gerald Wilkes of the Department of English, University of Sydney, for his helpful interest in the mss and to Mr. Malcolm Titt of Sydney University Press for giving so much of his personal time to its final presentation.

Perth   *Mary Durack*
Western Australia
1972

ACKNOWLEDGEMENTS

I wish to acknowledge the help I have received from Marjorie Rees. When Guy Howarth, then Reader in English Literature at the Sydney University, asked me to write this autobiography I began uncertainly and then became almost totally blind. Marjorie Rees immediately came to the rescue and gave me inestimable help, deciphering deplorable typing, sub-editing, reading aloud for correction etc. In fact, this book would never have been written without her skill and understanding.

M. L. Skinner

Sydney University Press gratefully acknowledges the assistance of the J. S. Battye Library of West Australian History in Perth in granting permission to reproduce seven photographs from its collection as the following plates: *The author, about the time of her meeting with D. H. Lawrence*; *Birthplace of Mollie Skinner*; *Sir John and Lady Winthrop Hackett*; *D. H. Lawrence's letter*; *South-west district hospital*; *Group Settlement in the south-west*; *A page from Mollie Skinner's unpublished novel.*

Are not five sparrows sold for two farthings?
Yet not one of them is forgotten by God.

Luke 12:6

1

Colonial Roots

My life began in 1876 in the Swan River Settlement of Western Australia when the colony was less than half a century old. I was born in the officers' quarters near Government House on the riverfront, with a cleft lip—but not a cleft palate, thank God. My mother, who had already produced in triumph a perfect son, was heartbroken at the sight of my defect. Afterwards she used to take me down under the trees by the river to nurse me, they say, alone with her sorrow. I was to distress her, one way or another, for the rest of her life.

As Jessie Leake, the lovely second daughter of a first settler's son, Mother reputedly could have married any one of seven dashing young men of that time. She chose my father, James Tierney Skinner, a captain of the 18th Royal Irish Regiment, the last officer to have charge of Imperial troops in Australia—and as poor as Job. He was the third of seven sons and one daughter, and he and his brothers all entered the army. Father had topped his final year at Sandhurst and risen quickly. He was the only one of the brothers with a head for mathematics, although four of them were colonels when they followed their mother's cortege to her grave.

My mother's family had numbered among the earliest in the colony, the first Leake to arrive having been her great-uncle George who left England in the chartered ship *Callista* in 1829, soon after the first contingent of settlers in the *Parmelia*. He brought with him sufficient assets in stock, grain, merchandise and indentured servants to entitle the family to a grant of 15,000 acres in the Upper Swan. His elder brother Luke, with their mother and George's fifteen-year-old daughter (whose mother had died when she was born), arrived in the *Warrior* in January 1830. Luke's wife, née Mary Anne Walpole, followed with three young sons in 1833, and in the next

1

year bore an only daughter who later became Lady James Lee Steere. The family decided quite soon to establish themselves as merchants in association with Lionel Samson of Fremantle and their first home was in that port. In 1835, however, Luke Leake and his family moved to a house in St. George's Terrace on the corner of what is now Howard Street.

Luke Leake's eldest son, George Walpole, my mother's father, was eight years old when he arrived in the settlement with his mama and two younger brothers. As most youths of well-to-do colonial families he was sent to school in England but returned at eighteen years old and studied law in South Australia. He was called to the bar in Adelaide, where he served for a while under Justice Boundy and married an English girl named Rose Ellen Gliddon who gave him seven daughters and two sons, one of whom died in early childhood while the other grew up to be State Premier. These children were all born in Western Australia where grandfather became the State's first Q.C., first Crown Prosecutor, and later Police Magistrate. I scarcely remember him but I grew up with his legend. They say he bore no trace of colonial background but was apparently the typical English dandy and socialite of his time, with a taste for high living, a sophisticated, often too caustic wit, and a prodigious memory for facts, faces, names and apt quotations. It seems he aspired to the position of Chief Justice of the Colony, but although he acted in this capacity several times he was never raised to that high office. He and his family had their own theories about this disappointment, though from less biased sources I gather that my grandfather was his own worst enemy. He could never resist the sarcastic rejoinder, the ironical turn of phrase that came so readily to his tongue. His quips and stories—often unfortunately rather coarse and locally known as 'Leakiana'—were quoted around Perth for many years after his death. The few anecdotes I remember do him rather more credit than otherwise and show him to have possessed considerable generosity. One concerns a man called Green who was brought before the bench on a charge of being drunk and disorderly. Sentenced to fourteen days, the fellow protested that he had been sold inferior liquor that had had an unexpectedly delayed action.

'Ah Green,' said my grandfather, 'I did not think you could be as green as all that.'

'That's as may be, sir,' replied the other, 'but I'm not so green as a leek.'

This flash of repartee was rewarded by a cancellation of his sentence and the payment of his fine out of grandfather's own pocket.

George Leake is reputed to have kept open house and would often surprise a newcomer by asking whether he had half a crown in his pocket. To the surprised affirmative he would reply: 'Well, keep it then and come to dinner with me.'

Grandfather called his seven daughters his 'seven disappointments' and when in a good mood, 'the Pleiades'. The eldest, Mary, was virtuous and married a bishop. My mother was naughty and fun-loving after her father's heart. They all grew up in a two-storey house with a shingled roof, originally built by the first Colonial Chaplain, the Rev. J. B. Wittenoom. It was set in a big garden that extended from St. George's Terrace almost to the river's edge on the site of what is today the Weld Club.

My mother and her sisters often recalled memories of their girlhood in that early-day Perth of sandy tracks and scattered houses divided by large areas of virgin bush. The amazing thing was that they managed to live with such refinement—even elegance—in this outpost of empire. The vast distance that separated them from the other Australian colonies had for them as many advantages as it had contrariwise. As people of a free settlement founded for the most part by members of the British landed gentry and respectable farmers, they had no great desire to associate with a mixed bag of 'jumped-up t'other siders'. Although the necessity of establishing themselves in a pioneering situation had forced our first families into middle class business and professional occupations they never forgot they had come of 'the gentry' and it was of the gentry they remained in their hearts. As soon as possible—and that was very soon indeed—they had built themselves comfortable houses on the English county pattern and surrounded them with gardens full of the flowers and trees of 'home'. All the early residences had their beds of pink moss roses, geraniums, verbena, mignonette, English daisies and rioting everywhere in the winter months masses of arum lilies, jonquils and narcissus. The settlers soon discovered too the advantages of their glorious Mediterranean climate and established long trellises of grapevines, planted mulberry, almond, quince and olive trees and grew stone fruits of all kinds. Grandfather George Leake had also impressive groves of bananas and plantains.

Mother often spoke too about the Aborigines, members of the local Bibbulmun tribe, who would wander into the garden—to the

considerable terror of servants not long from the old country—
wearing bones through their noses and flapping kangaroo skin cloaks.
In cold weather they carried their 'fire sticks'—smouldering hearts
of blackboy trees or dry banksia cones—and the women their 'cootah
bags' in which they swung their babies, with food they had gathered
—dug up, caught or begged along the way. They never stole but
always managed to go off with what they had come for, usually
matches and a sixpenny piece.

Grandfather George Leake was interested in—and amused by—
the Aborigines and enjoyed a rather incongruous friendship with the
Roman Catholic Bishop Salvado, a Spanish Benedictine who, when
he came to Perth from his Aboriginal mission at New Norcia some
eighty miles north, seems often to have dined with him. The family
would listen enraptured to the bishop's playing of the piano and
my mother recalled once hearing him give a pianoforte version of
a native corroboree, the manuscript of which he left with Grandfather. I wonder what became of it? It was remembered also that
Grandfather always obtained his olive oil from trees grown at the
Benedictine monastery at Subiaco, a few miles from the centre of
Perth.

In those days St. George's Terrace—now so smoothly macadamised
—was a lime-covered thoroughfare with a sandy track on either side
along which Mother, her sisters and their young friends would ride
their horses. A great sport of the time were paper chases, which
started from Government House, continued along the terrace uphill
to the Mount Eliza reserve and through the bush to 'the old tree'
somewhere on what is now known as Stirling Highway. While the
young people rode, the elders and younger children would follow
along in carriages.

Mother and her sisters often told how in November 1875 they had
stood on the balcony of Mr (later Sir) Frederick Barlee's house at
the east end of the terrace to witness Ernest Giles's survey party
crossing the Causeway at the end of their 2,500 mile journey from
Beltana in South Australia. These grave men, with their team of
twenty-four camels, were then on their way to a reception at Government House to which all the leading families of the colony had been
invited to follow them along the terrace. After the official speeches
of welcome the explorers had hoisted the ladies and their children
on to their camels and led them around Government House gardens,
with Governor Robinson's lady and her two daughters in the lead.

A corner of his property Grandfather had given over to a Miss Clay for a girls' school which was attended by his own daughters. The head—and only—mistress was an English gentle lady who set her pupils an excellent example of cultivated behaviour and gave them a surprisingly broad education. It was their father, however, who passed on to them a love of books along with something of his ready wit and sparkle. They were all lovely and consequently married young and, on local standards, successfully. When the youngest, my Aunt Blanche, was married to Dr Kelsall in 1892, her father apologised to the young men of Perth for being unable to provide them with any more wives.

In July 1872 mother and her sister Amey were double-wedded— at eighteen and seventeen years old. Aunt Amey's bridegroom was Henry Parker, a young lawyer who was destined for eminence in the affairs of the State. Naturally this wedding created quite a stir in local society. The reception was held at the Leake residence and my father's best man was young Weld-Blundell, aide-de-camp to Governor Weld and a prime mover in the formation of the Weld Club of which my father was at that time honorary secretary.

I was two years old when my father was recalled to England with the last remnants of the Imperial Troops that had served in the colony since the arrival of the first settlers. Officially the British troops had been withdrawn from Western Australia in 1863 but a few officers had remained in an administrative capacity connected with the pensioner force and the volunteers. My father, from the time of his arrival in Australia, had been Deputy Commissary for both Perth and Fremantle but this office was handed over to local government in 1878 and my father given an appointment with the British forces in Ireland.

2

Childhood

My mother, my elder brother Bob and I accompanied Father on the voyage. Of the sailing ship I remember only the smell of bilge and seasickness and feeling like a bubble risen to the surface when I was carried on deck and shown the great white wings held to the body of the ship by ropes.

We landed at Sherness, where my sister Estelle was born, and my brother, then three, went into sailor suits. I remember this giving me a twinge of envy, for it brought home to me that he was a boy and I a girl, that he was handsome and charming and much admired by everyone. I realised too that he came first with Mother as he would always do.

Later we went to London to visit my Skinner relatives. They were the stuff of Empire and of the class that referred to impoverished ladies of the upper strata as 'decayed gentlewomen'. Grandma Skinner had in fact been made a 'decayed gentlewoman' by her husband, an Indian judge who had left all his property to his only daughter, Minnie. This little aunt had been so small when born that it was said she could fit into a wine goblet. She remained tiny, never married, and ran the house in Grosvenor Place according to her dead father's wishes.

Mother said this elegant mansion with its four stories, attic and basement kitchen gave her the creeps. The staircase rising from the hall was dimly lit by a stained glass window above the first landing on which stood a glass case containing a stuffed white poodle. The softly carpeted drawing-room had tapestry covered chairs, numerous polished tables cluttered with ornaments, and cabinets crammed with treasures. A chandelier swung from the ceiling and the walls were hung with gilt-edged mirrors.

My grandmama, seated almost immobile in lace cap and cashmere

6

shawl in the midst of all this Victorian elegance, filled me with awe. Young as I was the sight of her and her surroundings made me suddenly homesick for my own country—a nostalgia I never lost until I returned to it. The only thing in the drawing-room that reminded me of home was the chandelier, which sparkled like the sunlit Swan River.

But in the kitchen I felt at ease, warm and happy, as I watched the sizzling joint turning on the spit before an open fire. I can remember demanding scrambled eggs and curry and the cook hugging me and letting me sit on the policeman's knee and trusting me to keep the secret of his being there. He was courting Emily, the parlourmaid, and once, when we met him on our daily walk, they became so absorbed in each other that I wandered off and got lost. Strangely enough, I was quite unconcerned, imagining the houses and streets to be the Australian bush where brilliant birds chattered, wattle dusted me with yellow pollen and the sunshine enveloped me. Then I saw a dog and thought it was the poodle in the glass case come to fetch me home. Hours later Cook saw my little fat legs coming up the steps to the front door and there was Aunt Minnie wringing her hands while a policeman took notes from a sobbing Emily. I remember this incident as the family never ceased to marvel that a child, not yet three, had found her way home in London. When I told them that the little dog in the glass case had fetched me back, they laughed, though I could see nothing funny about it myself.

When I was three and a half Father, now a brevet-major, was placed in charge of Fermoy Barracks, in Ireland. He must have been respected there for the colour sergeant once said of him: 'Where the major's boots are, there's his principles', which was high praise from an Irishman when the English were hanging men and women for the wearing o' the green. Indeed, it was a distressful country at that time. Landlords and officers too were constantly being shot from ambush and Father and Mother, returning from a party, were once held up but let go again.

Our home, at this time the only storied house in the barracks, had a walled garden and a nursery on the top floor by the maids' rooms which were unused as they were said to be haunted. Loubie, the nurse, slept in the nursery with us and I often saw ghosts after she had gone to sleep. They were tall, shadowy beings that wandered in and out through the closed door, and I liked them. One night when Father had gone to a mess dinner, the front door having been left on the latch for him to come in, the bell began to ring and ring. I heard Mother calling Loubie who jumped up, lit the candle and ran down to her. With the inquisitiveness of childhood I climbed from my cot and watched through the banisters. My father's voice boomed out: 'What on earth made you lock the door on me?'

''Twas the divil himself locked it, y' honour,' Loubie cried and when they came up Daddy was carrying Mother in his arms. My sister Muriel was born soon afterwards.

The raw Irish servants found my Australian mother hard to understand. Since she was not a Roman Catholic they dubbed her a 'heathen' and decided that, having come from that direful land of transportation she could not possibly know the manners of the gentry. Not that they knew them either, for we couldn't afford trained maids and Biddy the cook whenever Mother tried to explain things to her would take herself out into the garden and 'air her shroud'. Kate the housemaid when instructed to say that mother was 'not at home' to callers was heard answering the door with the words: 'Not at home, m'm—and may the Lord forgi'e me for the lie I'm after telling!' Another time when the General came to dinner Kate, asked to pay particular attention to him during the meal, kept digging him in the ribs and whispering in his ear: 'Are ye through, y'r honour?'

I see this period only in flashes, some clear, some shadowy. There were now five children—Bob, myself, Estelle, Muriel and baby Jack. I see Muriel stamping her foot at the servants and crying out: 'Call me Mittie Mollelle.' After that she came to be known as Mittie. I had become Mollie and Estelle was Stelle. When we went for walks we had a donkey with basket panniers for my two little sisters while Loubie carried the baby.

Bob and I did not go to school yet and were allowed to roam around the barracks where there was a fives court, rifle butts and a deserted ruin of a hospital inside the walls. The acrid smell of this place delighted me, and vaguely I imagined myself a nurse tending sick soldiers. Playing in the barracks yard in the open was no doubt, as Mother thought, good for us. Being thoroughly democratic, however, she allowed us to play with the barracks boys as well. These lads took us aside and unbeknown to our parents demonstrated the works of the devil, which remained hidden in the dark recesses of our minds.

What did awaken our elders to the dangers of freedom was that I, swinging on a water barrel on wheels, tipped the whole thing on top of me. Carried home for dead, I woke to show stormy resistance to being examined, naked, by three doctors. How I hated them!

Daddy made up to me with the present of an enormous wax doll and made me promise never to go outside the garden gates again unless with nurse. I obeyed him, for I loved him as I loved no one else. Mother once chastised me with a slipper, Father never. He always wore a red coat and I thought him beautiful until one day I burst into his dressing-room when he was bathing in his round flat tub. I thought him hideous. This was not the handsome soldier daddy who took me for walks over the emerald fields, pointing out primroses on mossy banks; not this the laughing hero who could toss us over the dining-room door and catch us on the other side; the man who smiled so engagingly when Mother accused him of being afraid to get up at night and investigate what haunted the house.

Mother was a streak of Australian sunshine, with soft sun-tanned skin and natural colour of lip and cheek, her melancholy, heavy-lidded brown eyes belied by her large, smiling mouth. She had perfect teeth and her nose and chin balanced the oval of a face capped by waving hair worn with a fringe. Her lovely hands were never, as far as I know, sullied by housework but, a born needlewoman, she made all her children's clothes. Everyone adored her and seemed to find her intriguing. Father's friends and relatives, hearing that he had married an Australian, expected him to bring home some sort of an Aboriginal, only to find her far more cultured than any of my uncles' English wives, always laughing and gay and completely at ease.

In 1885 father was promoted to staff major and ordered to Egypt to the Relief-of-Gordon campaign. Mother, determined to join him, took us to Buckinghamshire to a country house named Seven Oaks, kept by the Misses Bubb. Loubie addressed her tin box and sat on it on the Dublin wharf until put on the channel ferry for Liverpool where she sat on her box again until put on a train for Buckinghamshire. Mother then left Loubie in charge of the three younger children and took Bob and me to a widowed relative named Mrs Shiras in Edinburgh. When Mother returned to Seven Oaks to say good-bye to her little ones Loubie packed her box and went back to Ireland, but nothing could shake Mother in her purpose. She simply left her babies in charge of the Bubbs.

I felt no misery at parting from my parents. Mrs Shiras was kind and gave me a marble solitaire board to play with. Round and round flashed the blue Swan River, the green bush, the purple, red and yellow wildflowers, the rainbow-plumed birds . . .

Lizzie the maid slept in a box-bed that shut into the wall. She did all the work and on the rare occasions when Mrs Shiras went out at night entertained us by displaying the red hair on her bare legs. This she insisted we kept secret.

I attended a huge Academy for Young Ladies, walking from the flat in Dundas Street to Queen Street and back again daily. Bob, who went to George Watson's school up Castle Hill, had a much longer walk that weakened his constitution in the bitter Edinburgh winter on a bare Scotch diet.

My school, large and prosperous with classes of a hundred pupils each, was run by a Dr Pride. The elementary grade was divided into several sections and subsections but with a single teacher and one blackboard. The room was large and airy and full of eager little girls. At the beginning I was put at the bottom of my group but after the first terminal examination was moved to the top. I seemed to absorb knowledge without much apparent effort. I could do mental arithmetic with the utmost ease but was no good at sums on paper. Probably I was already half blind for I was also the worst copybook writer in the class, but having a vivid imagination could draw well. Music I never understood but was one of the three who led the choir of two hundred. I also led the drill and the dancing.

I loved my school companions and was popular with them, they said because I was 'different', with my Australian background and Irish brogue. I was always on my toes and dancing, quick to laughter, slow to tears, inclined to daydream but down to earth enough to enjoy ball games and racing. In winter when the rough boys made slides down the sidewalks on Dundas Hill I followed them without hesitation.

Previously Anglicans, we were Presbyterians at this stage and on one occasion I stood up at a revival meeting and boldly announced that I was 'saved', which made me quite a heroine.

So, for five years, I was an exceedingly happy child. I saw beauty which no one else could see, smelt things no one else could smell, and had no shame except for nakedness. I didn't believe a word of what other children told me of the facts of life, for a doctor had said he took babies to their mothers in his bag, which seemed much more credible.

What joy it was to be alive! When Mrs Shiras took us on excursions to ruined castles I saw them in my mind's eye peopled with knights in armour, ladies in high peaked hats and flounced skirts waving from the rough stone galleries, prisoners languishing in the awful dungeons.

In the holidays we were taken to Forfar by the Firth of Forth, where I was at once translated to Australia. The smell of new bread, the taste of honey, the aroma of the Firth were all Australian scents. I'd walk along the old, broken, weed-slippery pier above the quick-sands, and see in imagination black swans and sailing boats on sparkling blue water.

Bob was frightened and probably wished I'd fall in and be seen no more. He and I were good enough friends and companions, but not really close. He had Father's sweetness and Mother's sunny charm but as he was bored with all games except marbles he had few friends of his own age besides the arrogant sons of a doctor who lived in a grand street and never condescended to play in the Gardens with us. We considered it a privilege to go there, as this reserve was marked 'Private' and Mrs Shiras had a special key to it.

Sometimes we were allowed to go off alone to spend our penny-a-week pocket money and, when we were eight and nine, to take the cable tram to the big Botanical Gardens in Princess Street. It was there that I first sensed the existence of evil. We were one day admiring the flowers when we were accosted by an exquisitely dressed gentleman wearing yellow kid gloves and carrying a gold-topped cane. He told us that he knew a path up the Castle Rock to the bastion where the flowers were far better than down below, so up and up we climbed until the path ended at a bench backing a sheer cliff. Here the man sat down, took from his pocket a bag of lollies, began whispering to Bob, gave him sixpence and pulled off his horrible yellow gloves. That was enough for me. I swung my legs over the bench, pulled Bob so that he would have fallen if he had not come after me and over that cliff we went. How we got down safely I don't know, but I knew that man was the devil and that we had escaped a greater danger than we faced in eluding him.

By happy coincidence we ran full pelt into the arms of an officer we had known in Ireland, very big and grand in his Black Watch uniform.

'Oh, Fat Fitz, Fat Fitz,' I sobbed, "do you still love roley-poley pudding?'

We did not tell him why we were so delighted to see him and he didn't ask. But we told Mrs Shiras and she never let us out alone again.

Snippets of conversation, snapped off short when 'little pitchers with long ears' appeared, conclude that story: '. . . Yes, they caught him . . . it's in the newspapers . . . a monster like that . . . little children . . . deserves to be hanged . . .'

What is it that makes some people see beyond reality? That little girl had it. Queer . . . I could find lost things by closing my eyes. I could tell stories of times past back to the Roman empire and beyond, stories of shipwrecks and smugglers—things I had never heard of.

Once when I was given gas for a dental operation I apparently succumbed, but as I lay seemingly lifeless on the couch (the dentist no doubt in a panic and Mrs Shiras wondering how she would break the news to my parents) I was enjoying an extraordinary interview with an angel.

'You love life so much,' it said, 'but if you choose life the way is going to be difficult for you. The choice is yours. Do you want to come with me, or stay where you are?'

'I'll go back,' I said. 'I don't care how hard it is—I want to fight my life out.'

From that time on I was less joyous, less carefree. I became painfully conscious of my scarred lip and realised for the first time that there was a film growing over my eyes. A kind little girl friend assured me that I was not ugly, as I believed. She said my skin was like Rose-Red in the fairy story, my hair was pretty and my eyes blue as forget-me-nots. This comforted me a little but at the back of my mind there was a new and nagging fear.

I was nearly ten before Mother returned to England. Bob and I went down to Seven Oaks and there she was, with a new baby girl, my little sister Dollie. I rushed immediately to her beribboned cot and hauled her out to see whether her wings had disappeared (I doubt that they have to this day).

Mother was now thirty-three. Her lovely hair had turned white and she was more beautiful than ever, but she found her children had become strangers to her. Jack gave the most cause for concern, for he had grown into a strange, rebellious boy. Psychologists today would probably find that he had developed all sorts of complexes in his parents' absence. Stelle told us later that the Miss Bubbs had tied him under the yard pump and drenched him with icy water when he was naughty and that Annie the maid often threatened to give him to a policeman. He was ever afterwards afraid of policemen as of nothing else. He was given to screaming fits, during which Annie would lock him in the attic. As soon as she got downstairs again he would shout: 'Annie, Annie, I'm goin' ter be good.' But when she got up to let him out he'd say, 'I'm *not* goin' ter be good,' and start to yell again. Tired of his tantrums, Annie one day popped him over the garden wall into the shrubbery of Sir Austin Blake's estate, where he was found by the gardener, brushed down and taken to her ladyship who was having tea in the grand drawing-room. Suddenly Jack decided to turn on the charm. He told Lady Blake about his father who carried dispatches through the desert to the headquarters of General Gordon who was one day found killed by the enemy. And he told how Father, with his Arab servant and their two camels, had camped one night in the desert miles from anywhere. Father had placed his Wellington boots and sword at his side while he slept and when he woke his sword and one boot had disappeared, though fortunately not the dispatches he was carrying. This intriguing mystery was quite true and Lady Blake was suitably impressed. Mother heard afterwards that Jack had said he had been told never to ask for cake, but that if it was offered him he didn't have to refuse it. Altogether he had a most successful afternoon, but the gardener who brought him home delivered Mother a stern reproof for not taking better care of him.

Mother was not in the least concerned about this. In fact she took it as a great joke. Soon afterwards she packed up once more and returned with the baby to Egypt, leaving the rest of us in England as before.

3

Growing Up

When I was eleven years of age my father, now a colonel, was appointed second-in-command to Sir Evelyn Wood at Aldershot and he and Mother collected their children once more.

Our residence here was the finest after Flagstaff House. It was down below Gun Hill, on the fringe of a huge encampment, and was surrounded by a fine garden. The house consisted of three large five-roomed huts linked together in a U-shape. One wing was for parents and guests, the other for children and servants and in the central portion were the living-rooms. But as far I was concerned most of our life at Aldershot was literally blacked out, for I spent much of the time in a darkened room, my eyes bandaged and burning from ulceration of the cornea. My education, even such as I might have gained from reading, was therefore interrupted.

Two of my uncles were also quartered at Aldershot. Uncle Evelyn, the elder, whom we dubbed 'Mad, Methodist and Married', was in the Royal Engineers. He and his family were all so sanctimonious that when he retired later to Blackheath we referred to them as 'the Blackheathens'. Still, of all my relatives—except for my parents—Uncle Evelyn was the only one who was not frightened off by my darkened room. He felt it was his Christian duty to visit me, to preach and to pray, and although this bored me to distraction one little text reached out and touched my sleeping soul. It was from Luke 12:6. 'Are not five sparrows sold for two farthings? Yet not one of them is forgotten by God.' I came to see myself as the fifth sparrow—a poor, befeathered, blinded little bird yet still having joyful life, ability to fly, to sing, to preen, to pick up crumbs and drink and find fellowship with my kind.

Sometimes, after months shut away from the world, I would be allowed out, still bandaged, for walks with my sisters and their

14

governess. Occasionally I went with them to sports meetings in the officers' enclosure, to church parades and to gym, where I surprised everyone by my perfect marching. 'Toes out, stummocks in, head in air, arms swinging,' shouted the sergeant major. Mother protested that her girls were learning to walk like soldiers and not like young ladies, but Father insisted that it was good for Sally, as he called me.

And then there were the short, joyous intervals when my bandage was removed and I would go in the dog-cart with Mother for picnics by the canal. Uncle Edmund, Father's favourite and gayest brother, was usually a member of these parties. He had a rich wife and four little girls of whom he took not the slightest notice, but for some reason he was fond of me. He would choose the most beautiful lady at the picnic and go off with her in a boat, taking me along as chaperon.

With the onset of adolescence I longed for girl friends, apart from my sisters, but had found none since leaving Scotland. Bob was at school at Tunbridge and sometimes in the holidays I went around with him and his three boy friends. One of these was the General's son, Arthur, a gay lad full of pranks and laughter; another a quiet boy named Will Boyd, the only son of an adoring mother of whom he asked for five pounds to buy me a ring. Instead she got him to give me a Russian leather-bound Book of Common Prayer. This I still have, with his boyish inscription on the fly leaf: 'William Boyd to Mary.' It was my first lover's gift. But I was far more interested in the third friend, Robin Bruce Bryan, who was older and who later went with the Prince Imperial to the Boer War. There he was wounded and while crawling to give a drink from his water bottle to a fallen enemy he was fatally shot.

Freud might have claimed that I had a father complex at this time. I think it is more likely I had a mother one—in fact that we all had. Father was just someone my spirit reflected. Since early childhood we had all been parted from him while he was away doing his bit for Queen and Country. Now we grew to know him as if for the first time and found that the gorgeous uniforms were no more than a disguise for a very simple soul. Actually he hated them and liked nothing more than to get into shabby tweeds and with his old pipe gripped between his teeth to play cricket with us, teach us to ride, weed the garden, have us all around the table on Sundays while he carved the joint and in the evenings sing hymns with us around the piano while Mother played. He could curse and swear at Blackwell, his batman—who adored him—but the gentleness of his nature was revealed when he sang 'There's a Friend for Little Children', which was his favourite.

Those old hymns, so easily parodied and mocked, had a lasting influence on me. They soaked into my mind so that later in life the phrases served as ejaculatory prayers in dire danger, soothed me in anxious night watches with the sick, stood forth like swords against temptation. They were obviously written by people who had found refuge in God in bitter trouble and who bore witness that man's spirit could triumph over his mortal nature. 'Oh God Our Help in Ages Past . . .'

Father could never bring himself to raise a hand to any of us and Mother's pleas that he should take disciplinary action with Jack fell on deaf ears. Jack was Mother's thorn in the flesh, defying her at every turn, obstinate in the face of all her threats and punishments. He was sometimes put in bed in the spare room next to my dark one, his clothes taken away, and prescribed bread and water, but it was no use. Jelly the cook, a raw-boned, cussing sergeant's widow, was his faithful friend and would sneak into him with choice titbits from the dining-room.

Once he went off somewhere on his own in evil weather and was found, after a frantic search, drenched to the skin and up to his knees in icy mud. This escapade resulted in pneumonia, after which Mother decided that the only course was to whip him when he defied her. When Father refused to co-operate she took on the job herself and I was forced to listen to the battles that went on in the room adjacent to my own.

'Darling,' I would hear Mother say, 'I have to whip you and it hurts me more than it hurts you.'

'You try it,' Jack would answer.

It apparently hurt her so much that she persuaded the devoted Blackwell, father's batman and head groom, to perform the odious task—once. The performance over, Blackwell gave notice.

'Missus,' he said, 'tell the colonel I must return to the lines. You see, Missus, I can't do that again. Master Jack, he follows me down to the stable and gives me the only sixpence he has, missus, "to show there's no ill feelin'," he says, missus.' From my dark room I actually heard Blackwell sob.

For one of the few times in her life Mother was scared, for this gallant Tommy Atkins was the only person in the world who could dress Father properly for different occasions in his complicated red staff coats, frogged blue tunic, feathered cocked hat, sword belt, bandoliers, breeches and jack boots with stirrups. He was also the only one who would have put up with Father's awful cussing when he shaved in the morning and who understood the idiosyncrasies he had developed in his soldiering career. Besides all this Blackwell even turned out Mother's own dog-cart and acted as her groom, to the envy of all the other officers' wives. She begged him to change his mind, promising never to make such a request of him again. So Blackwell stayed.

For Jack's eighth birthday Father bought him a pony on which he rode to school. He was often late home after taking part in the rough sports of the soldiers, who adored him, playing rugger and cricket, joining in the foot races and riding exercises. No one objected to this and it no doubt helped to make a man of him.

I mention these incidents about Jack because years later D. H. Lawrence, watching him slouching down the path under the mulberry trees at Darlington, told me to use him as the hero of a book. *The Boy in the Bush* would never have been written if I had not known the boy Jack. Though born in Ireland, he was essentially a son of Australia, unbroken, free, courageous in his fight for his own individuality.

Bob, Mother's darling, was an individual too, but in a very different way. He loved—perhaps too fondly—the traditions of the Old World for their own sake and tried to remain wrapped in them after his return to Australia. He loved the Etons and tasselled mortar-board that comprised the Tunbridge uniform far more than the study required so that he could be articled to Mother's lawyer relatives in Perth.

Mother was ambitious for her children and hoped to make me a concert singer when I grew up. I had a choirboy's voice in those days, but no real sense of music or of the art of singing. A teacher was hired during this period to instruct me in the piano, but it was hopeless. Blindfolded, I sat there trying to practise but this caused me more agony than having my eyes cauterised. It was appalling for me too to have to sit through band concerts to which I was taken after visits to the occulist in London.

Mother said I would receive all the education necessary by sitting in the drawing-room on her days 'at home', listening to the conversation of clever and cultured people. My six years in Scotland repudiated this intellectual diet but I learned manners and social behaviour that served me in some stead in the years to come.

Then all at once I was sixteen and as suddenly I could see. To be released from blindness to light seemed like heaven and the world was mine. The utter joy of beauty! I could see the fruit trees in the walled garden, the hollyhocks, pansies and sweet williams, flox, stocks and Gloire de Dijon roses, the white blossom on the may tree, the purple leaves of the Judas tree.

My father was now transferred from Aldershot to take charge of Woolwich Arsenal where we were given a house at Eltham, near Shooters Hill, about five miles away. Here Daddy taught me to drive the gig and I took his precious mare over ruts and potholes; once, before he could stop me, over a foot wide hole in the street. I never forgot that because my usually gentle, humorous father was angry. He called me 'careless' just as Mother often called me 'clumsy', neither of them apparently aware that I still had only partial sight. I myself, not knowing that other people saw differently, did not realise it either.

But nothing could now dismay me for long. I started to write poetry and stories. As I knew nothing of verse form and was convinced that poetry must rhyme at all costs, the poems turned out as doggerel, and the stories, according to Mother, were nonsensical. Anyway, she insisted that it was only masculine women—like those silly hussies fighting for emancipation—who wanted to write.

It was that remark which first turned my attention to that gallant band of pioneers, including Dr Elizabeth Garrett Anderson, Lydia Becker, Barbara Bodichon, Emily Davies, and Beatrice Webb of whom everyone was so much afraid because although a lady she worked for the advancement of trade unions, rode a bicycle, ate bananas, skin and all, and made the Prince of Wales roar with laughter at his mama's receptions. How she got in at these I never knew because Her Majesty abominated these women who were trying to upset the Constitution, and especially those who espoused the cause of the trade unions. Life must have been full of shocks for the ageing Queen.

Now that I could read I devoured everything I could find about these brave women and the ideals they were fighting for. In my heart I wanted to be a nurse like my special heroine, Florence Nightingale, but hers was not a popular name at the War Office. When I broached the matter to Father he put his foot down and Mother did not try to change his mind. She was delighted when one day a famous musician who lived up the street heard me sing and came in to beg that he might teach me. Alas, in a week or so my voice cracked and Mother, realising that singing was not after all to be my career, persuaded Father to pay fifty pounds for me to attend the Buckingham Palace Road School of Cookery—a new feature attached to elementary education—and become a demonstrator. I failed to pass the theoretical examinations at this school. It's astonishing, in fact, that it was considered possible to pass, for one exam was on the chemistry of food, another on the theory and practice of teaching and another on housekeeping. But I was very happy during my time there. The other pupils were all older than myself and the chefs made a pet of me and oh, how I enjoyed the love and attention of girls of my own generation!

I thought a lot about love at this time. People talked of 'true love' and I wondered what it was. It seemed to be something that was considered rooted in marriage, but this I did not believe, as married people so often bickered and wanted to be divorced. Some said it was necessary to fall 'passionately in love' before getting married but from the French governess employed for our two babies I heard that in France marriages were arranged by the parents. It was all very puzzling. Stelle and Mittie, who had been sent to school in Belgium, told me that love was rooted in sex life which was necessary to reproduce one's kind, but I could not believe that this was its only purpose. I was sure there must be a sort of love that was far deeper and more profound than sex and was determined to find it. I said 'To hell with this sex,' and swore a solemn oath to remain celibate.

For a while I thought I would find all the fulfilment I needed in appreciation of nature—in the joyous flutter and songs of birds, the scent and fragile beauty of flowers, the new budding of apparently dead trees, the sun on the turgid waters of the Thames, in the slap of rain, in frosts and snow and ice on the pond where we skated in fullness of life. Then I remembered what the angel had said to me when I lay between life and death six years before: 'If you choose life the way is going to be difficult for you.' I had a feeling that the Being of the Voice was always with me—a Hand on my shoulder—and that it was urging me towards another and harder road.

By now I had acquired unknowingly a sixth sense given to the blind. I perceived by touch of hand and foot, by hearing, taste and my own emotions, and could often sense what a person thought was discreetly hidden—his or her real self. When I was confirmed it seemed clear to me that the Voice and the Hand were God's, that He loved me and had some special work for me to do. I longed to escape the restrictions of my home life and meet the neighbours He had bidden me to love as myself, but the people in our street did not want to be loved—by me at any rate. Surely, I thought, He must mean the poor, the lame and blind, the sick and downtrodden, and the best way to meet these was by nursing in a hospital.

It was at this stage that the spirit of the pioneers rose up in me. I told my parents that I was quite determined to be a nurse and that I believed it was my calling. Mother gave in first and Daddy, who was devoted to his Sally and hated the thought of the hard work I faced, eventually agreed to my entering for training at the Evelina Hospital for Children.

My career began when I was summoned to Broadstairs for a probationary period at the Metropolitan Convalescent Home for Children, where, for some unknown reason, the Matron took a strong aversion to me. When I bade her 'good morning' on first reporting for duty she glared into my smiling face and shouted like the Duchess in *Alice in Wonderland*: 'It's not the probationer's place to say "good morning" to the Matron. The Matron says "good morning" to the probationer—*if she chooses*!' The sparrow stood helpless, as though cornered by a cat.

Boils broke out on my neck and Matron burnt them with iodine forte. The sheer jumping torture of that! I mentioned this in letters home and also told of mental tortures inflicted on other young probationers who were wards in Chancery. Mother, in high dudgeon, took my letter to the Matron of the Evelina Hospital.

When called to the office one evening I sensed that I was for it. It is impossible in these days to realise the fury that some matrons of those times could unleash on their helpless subordinates. Not only did she tear out my feathers until I sank exhausted on the mat, but she abused my parents. 'Your mother,' she said, 'appears to be a typical product of transportation, raised from the gutter by an adventurous soldier of fortune. Let me tell you that whatever his position he has far less influence than I. At daylight there will be a cab at the door and off you go—back to your despicable family.'

I'll never forget Father's face when he saw his tortured sparrow.

Next day he put on his uniform and went off to interview the committee of the institution. It seems they received him with open arms, as so many wards in Chancery had come from the Convalescent Home with broken spirits but too frightened to confide their troubles. The Matron was summarily dismissed but this did not prevent her writing to the superintendent of every famous hospital in London, including of course the Evelina, warning them not to receive me as a probationer.

But the Royal Hospital for Women and Children in Waterloo Bridge Road, which was affiliated with the Greenwich Military Hospital, took me on as a guinea-pig (on payment of a guinea a week) and so I trained. The process, owing to my disability, was by no means easy. I learned to nurse mainly through my sixth sense and a feeling of brotherly love. I also found another outlet, and a little extra income, by contributing character sketches to *The Daily Mail* in London.

I had no sooner completed my course than it was decided that Mother should return to Australia with the family, to be followed later by Father. We sailed in the *Britannic* with show troops from a British regiment to parade before the Duke and Duchess of York at the opening of the Commonwealth. It was 1900.

4

My Australia—the 1900s

We tied up at Fremantle and there lay my fairyland in reality again. The new harbour had been completed two years before and the Establishment, as the prison was then called, still gloomed like a great stone fortress near the seafront. White-washed cottages, moss-grown and homely, side by side with more pretentious houses, lined the streets. Along the tree-dotted south shore were mercantile houses, business offices and a club and over the bar across the mouth of the Swan River the old wooden bridge, the sky and the sea like an iridescent bubble, and away inland the quiet grey-green of the bush. Fremantle, sun-drenched on its bed of silver sand, reminded me of the scene depicted by Lewis Carroll in 'The Walrus and the Carpenter'.

> The sea was wet as wet could be,
>   The sands were dry as dry
> You could not see a cloud, because
>   No cloud was in the sky.
>
> The Walrus and the Carpenter
>   Were walking close at hand:
> They wept like anything to see
>   Such quantities of sand:
>
> 'If this were only cleared away,'
>   They said, 'it would be grand!'

It was just like that.

And the air . . . the air was indescribably pure and sparkling with colour as if reflecting hidden jewels. It was air that healed sick lungs, brought joy to saddened hearts, lifted care from burdened minds.

We travelled to Perth on the railway that the people, after twenty

years, were still proud of having built over that twelve miles of sandy
scrub. Strangers sometimes laughed at the pride the colonials dis-
played in their progress, comparing their paltry development with
the wonders of the old world. It was difficult for newcomers to understand the sense of personal achievement felt by those who remembered
when it had all been virgin bush, challenging, formidable and
mysterious. But I understood this and I too felt pride in seeing and
hearing what had been done in a few short years. I thrilled to see
a growing network of telegraph lines and roads, breaking down the
terrible isolation, the fear of those vast and lonely distances. I viewed
with wonder the agricultural exhibitions and displays of stock, the
newly-established electric tramways and Royal Mint in Perth, the
Zoological Gardens across the river, the park on Mount Eliza, Queen's
Gardens at the east end of the town.

I listened with excitement to stories of the great gold discoveries,
to news of the passing of the Agricultural Bank Act, the sending of
a 'Bushman's Corps' to the war in South Africa, the establishment of
a butter factory at Busselton, the development of coal mines at Collie
—all the events and achievements that had swelled the population of
W.A. from 28,166 at the time of our departure for England in
1878 to a proud 179,967.

How lovely to be an Australian and young in this wide, free and
untrammelled land with its unique birds and flowers, its strange, shy
animals! Was there any other city, I wondered, so beautiful as my
birthplace, any water so brightly, smilingly blue as my own Swan
River, any port as fascinating as Fremantle, any land as ancient and
yet as new and undiscovered as this great western colony that was
soon, with the establishment of the Commonwealth, to become a
State? I loved it and had returned to it to find it more wonderful
even than it seemed in memory.

I found myself in a maze of relationships, our Australian cousins
numbering ten Parkers and ten Cliftons, three Lodges, four Parrys,
four Kelsalls, four Leakes—some grown up, some little ones. And
there were *their* cousins, and Mother's cousins and *their* relations
spread over most of the settled parts of Western Australia.

So much had happened in the family in the twenty-two years since
Mother had been out of Australia. Her father had died five years
before and I remember going with her soon after our return to visit
his grave in the little churchyard in East Perth, then surrounded by
bush. I was surprised to find how much of the history of the colony

—and of my own forbears—was to be found in that quiet God's acre surrounding the little timber church with its shingled roof and old bell swung from posts outside. Not only Mother's father, George Walpole, had died in her absence, but his younger brother, Luke, who had been the first Speaker in the Legislative Council. He had been knighted in 1876 after which discussions in the local Council became for the first time independent of the Governor, which meant that the colony was on the way to attaining responsible government. The two brothers who had played such a big part in the growing up of the settlement were buried beside their mother, Mary Ann Walpole, who had died a few years before I was born, and their grandmother, Ann Leake, who had arrived on the *Warrior* in January 1830 and died six years later. Hers was, I think, the oldest grave in that pioneer cemetery.

While Mother set to work to have a house built at Applecross Aunts Rose Clifton and Blanche Kelsall took us warmly to their hearts and made us feel at home, but the cousins, although they all admired Mother, were not too pleased at having five Skinner girls landed in their midst. There were three men to every woman in Western Australia at that time, but there was a dearth of beaux in society which was still very rigid and hidebound. The early settlers had produced about seven daughters apiece but so few sons that Grandfather Leake had been wont to say: 'It's nature adjusting herself to the conditions. Men come out in scores, and it's up to us to provide wives for 'em.'

Aunt Rose, sixth daughter of that 'fellow of infinite jest', was the bonniest, most delightful mother who ever helped to build a colony. She never went out of Western Australia in her life. There she sat in her hospitable home in Adelaide Terrace, darning and mending, always smiling, cheerful and contented, bringing up her brood of beautiful children. Her husband, Uncle Cecil Clifton, then Under Secretary for Lands and Surveys, was a grandson of Marshall Waller Clifton who arrived in Western Australia in 1841 with a group of settlers planning to develop the Australind district near Bunbury. The large-scale immigration project they hoped to launch came to naught but the scheme brought out a number of families destined to play an important part in the history of the young colony. These included the Forrests and the Johnsons—the latter a robust family of surveyors who became related to the Cliftons by marriage. Both Cliftons and Johnsons made their first homes on the estuary at

Australind, then a remote wilderness. Uncle Cecil spent much of his boyhood there and appears to have been educated by itinerant tutors. When quite young he had shown an exceptional aptitude for music and wanted nothing so much as to follow a musical career. As the family could not afford to send him away he had to content himself with a job in the Lands Department, while pursuing his true bent in his spare time. He was gentle and rather dreamy, and I don't know how he got as far as he did in the Civil Service, seeing that his mind was usually occupied with the problems of producing musical instruments. As a boy he had made a violin before ever having seen one—I believe the first such instrument in the colony. He had also, with the help of an Indian joiner named Hookham Chan, made the pipe organ for the Anglican Cathedral and we found him on our arrival at work on another one. It was a lovely thing, and still is. He later presented it to the University.*

All Grandfather Leake's seven daughters had married well and were in different ways remarkable. Aunt Mary had married Henry Parry who had been consecrated Co-adjutor Bishop of Barbados in 1868. He succeeded Bishop Hale to the Anglican diocese of Western Australia in 1877 and held that charge for eighteen years. Aunt Amey's solicitor husband, Henry Parker, was now a Q.C. and had been made Mayor of Perth in 1892. He later became Chief Justice and was knighted in 1908. After the formation of the Commonwealth, when Sir John and Lady Forrest made their headquarters in Melbourne, this aunt became the beloved leader of Perth society. But Mother, after her return, had the reputation of being the most beautiful woman in Perth society. People talked a lot about looks in those days—perhaps even more than today, when women are admired for a much wider range of attributes. Mother and her sisters were always compared to each other and to this one and that: 'How lovely Jessie Skinner looks in that frock, though Amey Parker looks beautiful too, of course.' We girls were always being compared or contrasted with our cousins: 'Funny that the Parker girls should be so much better looking than the Skinners, though their mother was the prettiest of all the Leakes.' I was well aware of the truth of this, as even our old cook, Cotter, used to tell us: 'None of ye'll ever ha' the looks of yer mama.'

* Robert Cecil Clifton wrote a paper entitled 'My Musical Instruments', Battye Library, W.A., PR 5129.

After my return I wanted more than ever to write, but no one was going to let me indulge this ambition if it could possibly be squashed. It was 'common', as nursing was 'common'. The only proper ambition a young lady was supposed to entertain was to secure a husband and in the process to look pretty and be as charming as possible. If she did not marry she was expected to remain at home and look after her parents until they died and then look after the old home until she died. It is surprising how many of the good-looking daughters of the proud Perth families did not marry and did just that! Most of my girl cousins seemed to concur with this view and wondered what on earth I had been doing with my time abroad that I should have come back with such a disappointing wardrobe.

'Haven't you any fashionable clothes to show us like your mother wears?' one of them asked me.

I looked her up and down with Victorian disdain. 'I have,' I said, 'a beautiful frock put away for the arrival of the Duke and Duchess of York.'

This was indeed a lovely dress and had been made for me by Mother's own fashionable dressmaker. It was white silk inserted with fine lace separated by minute tucks—all froth and billows, like gum blossom. How I looked forward to wearing this enchanting gown and how little I cared that I had so few smart clothes! Mother had a small private income from her father's estate but money was very short with us since all Father's savings were being put into the home going up at Applecross. Poverty, however, was of small importance to me, for little as we might have counted abroad, here we were of the highest in the land, the local aristocracy, while Father's having held positions of prestige and dignity in England gave us an extra feeling of superiority. In later years, after Father's death, I would many a time eat humble pie but I was far from humble then. Perhaps many young people, encouraged by their elders, still depend too much on their parents' status, to find out later that true prestige comes only at considerable cost and from one's own resources.

Most of the old 'first families' to whom, in their opinion, the West belonged, lived in stately colonial style in what was then Perth's most fashionable residential area—St. George's Terrace and Adelaide Terrace—in the vicinity of Government House. I often run along those thoroughfares in my memory, seeing the old homes and their residents as they were then. Uncle Henry Parker and Aunt Amey had a house on the corner of St. George's Terrace and Irwin

Street. Later the Celtic Club, it was then an impressive and hospitable home with a big ballroom, broad entrance hall and sweeping staircase. His brother George Parker had also built himself a big house close by on the corner of Victoria Avenue and St. George's Terrace, his property terraced down almost to the river's edge and including a tennis court. Farther along Adelaide Terrace were Aunt Rose and Uncle Cecil Clifton, Uncle George Leake, the Lee Steeres,* Wittenooms, Roes, Glydes, Hassells, the Stones of Rose Hill and the Burts of Strawberry Hill.

They all entertained a good deal and usually on a lavish scale too. They had servants of course—though they complained of how difficult they were to come by and usually how incompetent at that. This was not as true as it was to be in time to come but true enough to have made the women of these leading families extremely capable. The standard they kept up and their adherence to the old world protocol and etiquette was quite amazing. Between three thirty and five in the afternoon their carriages would be seen abroad as the ladies, in their beflowered and befeathered hats, gossamer veils and parasols, paid their formal calls or had their coachmen drop cards of reciprocal invitations on one another.

Vaguely I was aware of the tempo of political events in the background of our social lives. Sir John Forrest, who had been Premier for ten successive years, went to Melbourne as a minister in the newly established Commonwealth Parliament. My uncle, George Leake, became Premier. Women were given the right to vote; the goldfields were booming and pressing the government; C. Y. O'Connor, Engineer-in-Chief, was being politically badgered about his great scheme for carrying water by pipeline from the coast to the Coolgardie diggings, three hundred miles inland.

But I was too much otherwise engaged to think of these things as the historically important events they were. I was nursing, on and off, at Miss MacKimmie's private hospital in Havelock Street and was also enjoying myself immensely. As Bob's sister I was very much in the social swim. Everyone called him 'Popular Bob' and that is what he

---

* James Lee Steere named his house 'Eldersley' after a ship he had commanded before settling in Western Australia. The grander residence he later built opposite Government House was given the same name. He followed his brother-in-law Sir Luke Leake to the Speaker's Chair of the Legislative Council after the latter's death in 1886. He was knighted in 1888 and on the introduction of responsible government in 1890 became Speaker of the House of Assembly.

was—especially with Mother. He was not doing anything to further
his law career, but being good-looking, amusing, hail-fellow-well-met
with everyone from Government House circles downwards, his time
was fully occupied. Fortunately his gallantry extended even to his
sisters. He took us everywhere—admonishing us beforehand not to
speak with 'jam' in our mouths—and at balls always saw to it that
our programmes were full. Once I asked him why he didn't fill his
own programme first and his answer was typical. 'I keep it empty
until all the popular girls are dancing and the wallflowers are hoping
for someone to look after them.'

The people who gave us the best time of all were the Ogilvies,
a rich squatter family of 'the quality' who put their sons down for
Eton as soon as they were born. Mr Ogilvie (who was later drowned
on his Murchison station) and his beautiful wife always stayed, when
in Perth, at the Palace Hotel. Here they entertained famous visitors
passing through on their way to the other States and Bob and I were
often with them. It was in this circle that I met that charming
scientist, Professor Frederick Soddy, who, then only a young man,
was already carrying out research in the field of radio activity, a work
for which he was to win the Nobel Prize in Chemistry in 1921. He
has no doubt forgotten me long since, but I remember him for he
took me to realms of wonder far beyond any reached through his
public lectures. He carried with him a small piece of radium that one
could see, mysteriously, through the covering of its box.

At the races, to which Bob and I drove with our friends in their
four-horse coach, I could always borrow a sovereign from Mrs
Ogilvie knowing that she would take it back without embarrassing
me, which meant a lot to one who was young and shy and full of
rectitude.

As the great day drew near for the arrival of the Duke and
Duchess of York and invitations were being prepared for official
functions there was a hasty weeding out of citizens of convict descent
and others not considered socially acceptable. The free-spending Mayor
of Perth, Mr W. G. Brookman, had made his pile on the fields and
had stood for the mayoral election of 1900. Some of his proposals
were truly visionary and included finding a new site for the Perth
Town Hall, widening Hay Street and building a bridge across the
Swan River Narrows. However, not being connected by birth with
the First Families, he was considered 'unsuitable' and was suddenly
removed from office and Uncle Henry Parker put temporarily in his

place. He took their Royal Highnesses everywhere, Bob in a top hat following after with his eternal grin.

How I laughed at the discomfiture of the A.D.C's when the Perth ladies bobbed instead of curtseying, and turned their backs after being presented! As one of them, very flustered and excited, was heard to remark: 'I'm not falling over my train by walking backwards for anyone.' Amusing too it was to watch people hastily taking off their gloves before shaking hands with the royal guests at the garden party, and to listen to the endless post mortems that went on long after the royal visitors had returned whence they came.

Much as I revelled in all these happenings, my greatest thrill of that year was winning second prize for a Christmas story in the *Western Mail*, second prize in an English journal *The Hospital and Nursing Mirror*, and first prize for a story in a country newspaper.

Before leaving England I had been sent for by the Benson brothers, authors of those best sellers of the day *Dodo* and *The Dolly Dialogues*, who had just started a periodical for colonial distribution. They had heard of me somehow as an aspiring writer and engaged me to write an opening article for their magazine on our voyage in the *Brittanic*. This had since appeared, to my great delight, though not to Mother's (or that of anyone else as far as I know) and as the periodical died bankrupt in infancy I was never paid for it.

So now I knew that I could write and that it didn't pay. But it paid my heart, particularly when a patient at a hospital where I later nursed showed me an unsigned story in the local *Daily News*. 'That,' she said, 'was taken from a London newspaper. I think it's splendid.' I took it and found that it was my own. I thought Mother would be pleased to hear of this, but when I told her she grimaced as she did when the dog brought her some old bone it had dug up in the garden.

Mother's dream home over the river at Applecross was an eight-roomed house of beautiful timber, plastered and with great windows a couple of feet from the floor to display the glorious river view. Complete with all the latest conveniences of those times, it was ready within a few months. From there we crossed to the city and back in the old paddlewheel ferry which took half an hour each way and also made regular trips to Coffee Point and Canning Bridge.

A boy friend once persuaded me to sail to Applecross on his yacht. A sudden gale blew up and I grabbed the tiller—he said nearly capsizing the boat; I said, saving the situation. As neither of us would give in and we could not swim anyway, that was the end of the affair.

Although conventional in some ways, Mother felt we should all be able to earn our own living. Perhaps she saw this as a necessity. She said she didn't want any of us to marry and she took over every young man we ever brought to the house. They simply fell in love with her and that was the end of our chances.

Daddy came home in 1902, knowing, as we discovered later, that he was soon to die, but telling none of us. He played bridge with us at night in the beautiful drawing-room with its furnishing of Egyptian rugs, divans, brass trays and miniature mummies that he and Mother had procured in Egypt. Only just over fifty, he would have preferred to retire in England as his English ways were all wrong here and he missed the friends of his youth. He had given Mother his every penny to build the house and did not even complain about her choosing a locality where there was no golf course. He was distressed about Bob who never worked, and about Jack who he feared might be going to the dogs outback, and Estelle who was always defying Mother, and I suppose one way or another about us all. What had he to live for?

When he collapsed one night our only neighbour came in and held a looking-glass to his lips and said we must send for a doctor. Uncle Harry (Dr Kelsall) came at once and broke it to us that Daddy was dead and that he had known the end would come at any time.

Looking at him lying there, so still and at peace, I realised it is not death one needs to fear. I thought of the famous epitaph written for the Earl of Devon in 1419:

> What we gave we have,
> What we spent we had,
> What we left we lost.

The coffin was carried to the ferry and he went away over the blue water to be buried at the new Karrakatta Cemetery,* his grave heaped with flowers. I have hated wreaths and crosses of flowers ever since. 'What we gave we have' was enough for me.

---

* Burials in the pioneer cemetery in East Perth were discontinued from 1899.

5

Perth in the New Century

Mother had chosen for Father's tombstone the words: 'Behold I come quickly', but as my brother Jack shrewdly observed, she had no intention of doing so.

Father had made me his executor together with one of Mother's lawyer relatives but Mother did what she liked with both of us. Despite her private income her affairs had always been one with Daddy's and the small estate took some time to rearrange. All I contributed to the transactions was to go with Mother and sign papers at the lawyer's office, but the thirty pounds I had saved from my earnings kept the household going in the meantime. I did, however, reserve seven pounds from this sum to buy myself a secondhand typewriter—which Mother considered selfish and unnecessary. I argued in vain that the novel I was writing might one day help support the family. It didn't, of course, for though I finished it it was never published and has long since disappeared. I never even learned to type properly.

It was a hard time for us all, as Mother's brother, the Premier ('Young George Leake' as he had always been called to distinguish him from his father of the same name) had died in office just before Father, so we had lost our two main supports at much the same time. Bob was no help. In fact, almost everything Mother had from this time on she spent to save him from the disgrace of debt. Jack, still only seventeen, was more independent, but his earnings were barely enough to keep himself. Father had paid the usual fee for him to learn farming with Uncle Tom Lodge (a cousin of Sir Oliver Lodge) and Mother's sister Aunt Connie on their property at Beverley. He had remained with them a year, until their house was burned down, and he had then gone to work as a jackaroo on a station in the north-west. We had not seen him since our return to Australia but

31

soon after Daddy was buried he turned up, to our astonishment, a disreputable ulster flapping over his dungarees and vest.

'Darling,' Mother greeted him, 'where did you get your fare down on the steamer?'

'Worked it,' Jack said. 'The chap who was going to bring sheep down for the boss got dead drunk in the port so he gave the job to me. I hand-fed the bleating blighters all the way, stayed in the stinking hold with them, held 'em up when they fell down and I never lost one of 'em. How's that for a blinking wonder, eh Mum?'

'But dear,' Mother protested, 'you can't go about dressed like that! We sent you out to Australia with corduroy breeches, silk shirts and Harris tweeds. What *have* you done with them?'

' Lost the lot in the Lodges' fire,' he said. 'Jolly good job too.'

'Oh . . . how incorrigible you are, Jack—not improved in the least. Well, borrow something of Bob's . . .'

'Jesus Christ, I wouldn't be seen dead in Bob's togs, Mum.'

'Don't call me Mum. I can't bear it—and please refrain from blasphemous language.'

'You taught me to pray at your knee, didn't you? And now when I pray you call it blasphemy.' Jack went on his way, whistling.

Although he was a trial, as ever, to Mother, we girls adored him, but he was soon off in his old ulster to the goldfields—'to knock up a cheque, Mum,' as he said. And Bob went with him.

Bob was soon back, saying he was ashamed of Jack who mixed with the scum, ran foot races, gambled, drank, did double shifts on a windlass and spent what he made drinking and shouting his mates. Poor Bob never made anything and what he borrowed he spent at the pub at Canning Bridge on the back-track to Fremantle. One day Mrs Quigley, the proprietress, came over to fetch Mother and the two of them shepherded Bob—the precious black sheep—away from her cheery premises.

It was Bob far more than Jack who was incorrigible. He'd pick and arrange flowers for Mother in the morning, then nip off and do the same for Mrs Quigley at the pub. Back for dinner, he'd entertain Mother with gossip from Town, and then he'd be off again when she was having her siesta. Back again for high tea, he would play the piano for our evening hymns.

But he was not despicable and it was impossible not to love him. He himself loved everybody and gave credit to others for their intellect and good works. Simple and sincere, when he sang those hymns he meant them with all his heart. He simply hadn't the courage to master his weaknesses. He feared pain and believed that moral strength would cause him unutterable suffering. He also believed it the duty of all of us to see that he was called upon to suffer as little as possible. He would yell with anguish if the bottom blanket was not put on his bed. 'You have to have as much blanket under you are over you or you'll get rheumatism,' he'd say. And he would behave with offended scorn if his underwear was not ironed, or his shorts not starched. 'How *can* you expect a fellow to be a gentleman, if you don't do anything for him?'

When he returned from the 'fields Bob was shoved into a government department and had lodgings in Perth where his landlady adored and took care of him, as all women did. His men friends too looked after him till they could do so no longer—helped him from the gutter when he was drunk as a lord, washed, shaved and dressed him, and at least once sent him off to a dinner at Government House as fresh as the bunch of wildflowers he handed with his charming grin to Lady Bedford. He had gathered them during the afternoon and placed them in water, before his drinks.

This could not last. He was woefully in debt and Mother had all she could do to pay his creditors and hush-hush him into the country.

Estelle went into the telephone exchange, Mittie looked after the home, the two younger girls went by ferry daily to school in Cathedral Avenue. I had a telephone installed so that doctors could call me for private nursing jobs, though as I now only wanted to write, I loathed the idea. Something in me demanded my own individuality and the opportunity to watch my beloved land as it developed from colony to state.

Motor cars had now made their appearance and Uncle Harry Kelsall took me with him when he was trying out one he had bought for himself. It was the second or third on the roads around Perth and was like a two-seated carriage with a tin box on the back. The passengers sat behind a splashboard, the driver holding a stick like the helm of a yacht. Confronted by the steep incline of Malcolm Street, Uncle Harry bade me get out and walk to the top to lighten the load. Even so, he would never have made it without the help of passers-by who pushed, strained and sweated at the back, almost falling flat on their faces when the car made off with a sudden spurt at the top. Afraid to stop, or forgetting how to, Uncle Harry, his teeth clenched and turning so sharply that he nearly capsized, shouted to me to jump in for the perilous descent. 'If the brakes are no good,' he yelled as I plonked down beside him, 'we'll land in perdition together.'

I always remember sailing down that hill in joyful exhilaration, the view of greater Perth disappearing as we descended towards the Barracks.

Uncle Harry was a delightful character. I thought him probably the most entertaining member of the family and I never tired of listening to his stories. Born at Nani Tal while his father was a surgeon major in the India Army, he was educated in England where he qualified as a doctor and served as house surgeon at Moorfields Ophthalmic Hospital. During this time he made a number of interesting lifelong friends including Sir Rudyard Kipling and Sir Wilfred Grenfell of Labrador with whom he worked for a while as M.O. on deep-sea fishing boats. For a time he also acted as ship's surgeon in the Royal Navy but was soon persuaded by his medico friend Dr Thomas Frizell to take over his practice at a fascinating place called Roebourne in Western Australia. I don't think Uncle Harry could have found Roebourne as delightful as his friend made it out to be for he soon left and went into general practice in Perth, married Aunt Blanche and later decided to specialise in ophthalmology.

He was a man of many and varied interests and sat on more committees than I can attempt to remember. I do know, however, that he was a trustee of the Art Gallery, Museum and Public Library and a member of the Acclimatization Committee then in charge of the South Perth Zoo. He was the President of the Perth Rifle Club and was also a keen cricketer, tennis player and fisherman.

He had a great reputation as an oculist and as an honorary at Perth Hospital tended the eyes of the roughest labourers as meticulously as those of his highest paying patients. I cannot understand how he never noticed that I was three parts blind. Perhaps he did, but knowing that glasses would not help my condition, decided that to inform me just how poor my sight was would have taken away much of my confidence.

He did not appear to notice either that the old order was sinking into obscurity. He found it as hard as any other early settler to realise that although the big gold rushes had now subsided, the 't'other siders' whom they had encouraged to the West had come to stay and were already changing the English landed gentry character and standards of the early years. Like most members of the First Families he tried to shut these newcomers out of his mind, at first believing that sooner or later they would pack up and go back where they belonged. But this was not to be. It was the fading hour. It was 1903.

My mind, as the Crown colony days gave way to the new order, was as raw, politically and economically, as that of most girls of my time. I did feel, however, that it was wise for our little world apart to join hands as a Commonwealth with its sister States—in fact to be ruled from Melbourne (Canberra being scarcely thought of then) instead of Downing Street. On this issue there was a cleavage between myself and some of my maternal relatives who wanted things to stay as they were. But my Uncle George Leake had always been one of the colony's keenest supporters of Federation; in fact it was he who had urged a referendum on this issue in 1899.

In spite of the prosperity promised with Federation and the gold that had brought fame to the Western State many things, dearer to the local people than progress, were already slipping away. Everything seemed muddled, contradictory and, to the older people, deplorable. In the previous year the Engineer-in-Chief, C. Y. O'Connor, hounded by criticism and doubt of the great water scheme that was to mean the life of the goldfields, had died by his own hand. With the death of the Premier and my own father later in the same year, it seemed to me that an era was dying too.

Everywhere new houses were being built for strange identities— the newly-rich from the goldfields—to us mere nobodies no matter how much money they had or how much they flaunted their banners of 'speculation', 'finance' and 'business acumen'. My distaff forbears had passed on to me a great love of everything connected with the early days of the colony. I loved—and still love—the old Town Hall, built by the convicts in the short eighteen years of their transportation to Western Australia, the little slit windows shaped like broad arrows in the tower; the old post office behind it, facing the broad Terrace; the Anglican Cathedral; the quaint old Deanery beside that—and so much else. Although before returning I had known this place only during the first two years of my life, I seemed to remember it as it had been, and part of my dreaming mind remained faithful to it.

I was young and objective enough to realise that these t'other siders, coming in with new blood and new ideas, treating our Cinderella state as though of equal standing with her more prosperous sisters, must help the development we so badly needed. But I was also very conscious of the fact that few of the newcomers were our social equals.

My first close brush with one of the new-rich couples was when I was called on to nurse a woman who had suffered the passing of a gallstone. She was over the worst before I arrived, but insisted that I lie on the bed beside her and stroke her head, and before I left she gave a tea party to show off her nurse who was from 'one of the Old Families'. I was bidden to set out her special tea service and in doing so I broke a cup. When I confessed she sat for some time in stony silence.

'I'll buy you another,' I said, in an agony of embarrassment.

'Impossible,' she replied. 'Those cups are priceless.' She fell silent again, explaining some time later, 'I always keep quiet when I'm upset—until I get over the shock.'

Later in a shop I saw identical cups and saucers selling at seven and sixpence each.

When I went to collect my fee of two and a half guineas her husband handed me two pounds ten, saying, 'Guineas are illegal.'

But I had seen enough of life to realise that the distinguishing marks of quality were not a matter of social station so much as of innate good taste and sensitivity. How different was Sir John Forrest —our own 'Jarrah Jack'—who of robust Scottish stock was so fine a gentleman. People of vast intelligence can never fathom why he grew so great, and some have the temerity to say he wasn't great at all. They say he plucked the ideas of his friends to make his own laurel crown, but he did nothing of the sort. He simply combined the leaves of others—like the shamrock of C. Y. O'Connor—with the foliage of his own jarrah. Together Forrest and O'Connor had brought to fruition the harbour, the railways and the Coolgardie Water Scheme—achievements which neither could have accomplished without the other. Granted, it was the great engineer who planned and constructed the projects but it was Forrest who had to move an obstinate, lethargic, stagnated population to provide the funds.

People said: 'If only he'd used finesse, had been less sentimental, shown a sense of diplomacy, an insight into human nature, he might have been really as great as he had the chance to be.' But if he had *not* used finesse, his knowledge of the country and the people he had known from earliest boyhood, he could never have risen to be the first Premier of the colony, to hold that position for ten years and to relinquish it only to become a Federal Cabinet Minister and then to be created Australia's first baron—Lord Forrest of Bunbury.

I remember so well visiting the Forrests at their home, 'The Bungalow', in Hay Street—long since demolished. It was in 1903 and they had come over from Melbourne to open the Coolgardie Water Scheme.

We sat in the garden, John with the beard and the too large corporation common to so many men of that time. Holding the cup of tea his wife had poured for him with her haughty and delicate air, he chuckled with me over what we both thought his greatest achievement—having had published the accounts of his expeditions. These journals* were terribly entangled with notes on the stars that guided him, the sufferings of his horses, the vegetation, geological formations and the like. Most of the writing was as flat as the landscape he had traversed but to me it created vivid pictures of the vast, empty background of the State. With eager questions I persuaded him to enlarge a little on his text but he found description difficult. Talking was never his strong point. His public speeches were monotonous and everyone went more or less to sleep until he thundered forth his favourite words: 'This is a land of opportunity, progress and eventual prosperity. It is the Coming Colony—but if we are half-hearted, if we are faltering in any way and show ourselves weak, we will never progress . . .'

John Forrest was then over fifty, but as we sat there under the trees outside his home his mind ran back to when he was a young man, lithe and splendid in his male pride and belief in himself. He recalled setting off in 1869 with George Monger, Malcolm Hamersley, a smith to shoe the packhorses, and two Aborigines, one of them Tommie Windich who was to accompany him on many later expeditions. Their objective was to investigate a native's report that the bones of the explorer Leichhardt lay bleaching in the sun where no white man's foot had ever trod. I seemed to be with the party when they lay under the stars at night, shot wild fowl and made damper, trod over lumps of gold, tramped past rocks impregnated with precious stones, battled over treacherous saltwater lakes, wondering if they were part of an inland sea, found water in rock-holes and

* *Journal of an Exploring Expedition to the country eastward to Port Eucla and thence to Adelaide* (1870), *Journal of the Proceedings of the Western Australian Exploring Expedition through the Centre of Australia* (1875), *Explorations in Australia* (1875), *Notes on Western Australia* (1884).

native wells (hidden soaks), chased after smoke from natives' fires, came once or twice in weeks on furtive Aborigines. Once it was an old man left to die in the arms of a silver-leafed tree; once an Aboriginal holding the hands of his two little children, so smitten with grief that he did not see the exploring party. Then, the tears streaming from his eyes, he told of wild natives who had killed and eaten the children's mother, and so he was taking them to his tribe.

. . . It is a few years later now. His brother Alec is with him traversing the south coast to survey the telegraph line . . . Later again they are dragging weary dogged limbs over the desert that had eluded the eye of inquisitive white men for countless ages.

'Anyway, it won me my wife,' said Sir John.

'And fame, my dear,' Lady Forrest added. She turned to me: 'You know I suppose, Mollie, that he was afterwards proclaimed a great explorer and he went to Europe. It was on his return that he began his political career.'

After he left us to attend to his affairs of state Lady Forrest pressed me to stay and talk to her. I was flattered and rather awed, remembering all the things I had heard of her. My mother had known her when she was Margaret Hamersley, daughter of old Edward Hamersley of the Council who had come out from England in the early days and planted a vineyard at Guildford. His wife was French and her mother was said to have been a royal child smuggled out of the Tuilleries by her nurse after the fall of the Bastille. The Hamersleys had brought their daughter up as if *she* were a princess. She received a broad education, became a talented pianist and painter and was the natural leader of the younger set in the colony. She was besieged by suitors and flirted with them all, though supposed to be half engaged to Maitland Brown, that elegant young leader of the north-west squatters. She always seemed to stop at the point of committing herself and then it began to be whispered that she seemed unaccountably smitten by a hobbledehoy named John Forrest who was attached to the Lands Department.

Mother said it was Margaret who taught John good manners and gave him any culture he possessed. It may have been so, though I myself believe he was a gentleman born. Perhaps, however, it was his eagerness to please and so live up to his haughty, cold and possessive wife that impelled him to the forefront of public life. She was certainly a great social asset and a wonderful hostess, practised in all the niceties of those formal days. Their home was not one of the grand mansions such as appeared in Perth after the gold rushes but it was furnished with impeccable taste, as nearly as possible after the style of the Hamersley home, Pyrton Manor, in Oxfordshire, England, and with a special gallery in which hung Lady Forrest's own botanically perfect paintings of the State's unique wildflowers and blossoming shrubs.

Being asked to stay on alone with her made me rather nervous for no woman ever really felt at ease with her. She was not at all gushing, never spiteful, but inclined to seem, on first meeting, rather cool and condescending. Soon, however, I got over my shyness and really enjoyed myself, for Lady Forrest numbered among her many accomplishments the gift of telling a story well and with spontaneous flashes of humour. She spoke of the exciting growth of the colony since the discovery of gold in '92, the spread of our railways and telegraph lines and the opening of the goldfields water supply when boys dressed in white sailor suits had pulled Sir John and herself through the streets of Coolgardie in a cart decked with flowers—and how she laughed as she recalled how a group of Aboriginals, standing stark naked as they passed, had called out 'John Forrest—he my father!'

I was to meet the Forrests often during this period but this day at the old Bungalow remains as something special in my memory.

6

The Hacketts

Perth in those early days had many vivid personalities, but the two who—to me—most personified confidence in individual living were John Winthrop Hackett and his wife Deborah.*

He had something hard to describe, this man; something almost biblical in kindliness, humility and spiritual power. He loved his neighbour as himself and was free from any taint of jealousy, rudeness or self-glory. If he believed he was right he took not the slightest notice of either praise or blame and proceeded without confusion to carry out his plans. He was indeed a very *parfit gentil knight*. I am sorry for those who did not realise his greatness when he lived amongst them.

Born in County Dublin, Ireland, in 1848 and educated at Trinity College, he practised as a lawyer in Sydney and later in Victoria before coming to Western Australia in 1882.

The old colonials cared nothing for the degrees he bore and with typical parochialism the people of Perth had not at first taken him very seriously. But John Winthrop Hackett was loaded not only with intellect, but with tact, good humour and the spirit of youth, even

---

* John Winthrop Hackett (M.A., Hon. LL.D., Trinity, Dublin, 1902) was knighted in 1911, created a K.C.M.G. 1913. He married Deborah Vernon Drake-Brockman in 1905 and had four daughters and one son. He was President Perth Public Library, Museum and National Gallery; Registrar of Anglican Diocese and Chancellor of St. George's Cathedral; first Chancellor University of Western Australia when opened in 1913 and himself endowed a Chair of Agriculture. When Harper died in 1912 Hackett assumed full control of *The West Australian* and the *Western Mail*.

Hackett died in Perth in 1916. After providing for his family he bequeathed money for the building of St. George's College, the first residential college in Western Australia, the residue of the estate being left to the University which received £425,000. Another £200,000 provided scholarships, bursaries and financial help for deserving students.

if the tact was subtle, the humour Irish, and the spirit of youth absurd —to them.

Soon after his arrival in Western Australia he had gone up north on a sailing ship, bought a sheep station and returned to Perth saying he would be back north in time for the lambing. When he received a telegram informing him that the lambing season had begun he was said to have wired back: 'Put it off.'

One disastrous season convinced him that the land was not his forte and he abandoned the project and joined Charles Harper, proprietor of *The West Australian* and *The Western Mail*, as assistant editor of the latter paper. In 1887 he became editor of *The West Australian*, in which capacity he was a strong supporter of responsible government which status was granted to the colony in 1890.

In 1894 he was elected to the Legislative Council as Member for the South-West Provinces which he represented until his death. Although often asked to join various ministries he believed that his main mission lay in his newspaper work and at the time of our return to Western Australia he was mainly absorbed in the editorship that had done so much already to influence the outlook of the community. He strongly supported Forrest's developmental policies including the Fremantle harbour scheme and the goldfields water supply and, a staunch advocate for women's suffrage, was largely responsible for the Western Australian government being one of the first in the world to grant women the vote.

He was not good-looking, his features behind the well-trimmed beard and moustache not of much distinction, but his figure was lithe and slim, his hands slender and strong, and he was always well and conservatively dressed. His laugh seldom rose above a chuckle and his clear melodious Irish voice was part of the secret of his extraordinary charm. He was, however, something of a recluse. Few people were on intimate terms with him and most were more than a little in awe of him. No one, as far as I know, ever called him John except his wife, but he had the power of inspiring many he met with a passion for culture and a desire to further it in the young State.

In his three-storied house in St. George's Terrace at the foot of the Mount, he entertained with old world courtesy and lived, as far as possible, the life of an Irish gentleman. That is to say, he employed a staff of servants under a housekeeper, had a well-appointed dining-room, an elegantly furnished drawing-room and a private study. He also kept a carriage and coachman to take him to and from his office.

Apart from big functions he was little seen socially and he was, it was thought, a confirmed bachelor. Then, to everyone's amazement, he began courting a seventeen-year-old girl named Deborah Vernon Drake-Brockman, daughter of a leading surveyor and a member of the pioneering Bussell family. Her mother, Grace Bussell, had made a name for herself as a girl of sixteen by riding her horse into the raging surf near the mouth of Margaret River to rescue the passengers of the wrecked ship *Georgette*. She was hailed as 'Our Grace Darling' and together with the native boy, Sam Isaacs, who assisted her, had been honoured with a presentation from the Royal Humane Society. Grace was not much older when she married young Fred Drake-Brockman.

All the family of that couple were remarkable. Edmund became a major-general and Chief Justice of the Federal Arbitration Court, Geoffrey a brigadier and highly placed engineer in the Civil Service, Karl a Rhodes Scholar and lawyer, Alan a successful businessman and judge of dogs. Besides Deborah there were the beautiful twin girls, Rica and Enid, whose heads were as fair as Deb's was dark.

As an intimate friend of that family I remember the disapproval they expressed when Deborah, scarcely out of the schoolroom, announced her intention of marrying the enigmatical Dr Hackett. No matter how brilliant, wealthy and charming he might be the fact remained that he was not a member of one of the State's precious 'first families' and no one quite knew what he was about. Riding together through the bush near her parents' home at Guildford she confided in me about her romance. 'If John were a sweep I'd love him,' she declared. 'No matter what anyone says we're going to be married and live happily ever afterwards.'

Deb was one of the most beautiful creatures ever born in the State—or anywhere else for that matter. I never knew another with the fire, classic features, dark blue eyes, raven hair and quick mentality of Deborah. How wild she was, galloping heedlessly and fearlessly through the scrub, while I, unused to the rough going, followed as best I could, aching in every limb.

She spoke no less than the truth, for she was deeply in love with her John and he with her and they were married in 1905. Far from losing my friend as I feared, this marriage gave me another whose memory I was to revere.

The hours kept in the Hacketts' home were unusual. Dr Hackett went to his office during the afternoon and again after dinner until

2 a.m. The housekeeper continued to run the house and an English nanny presided in the nursery—for Deb was the mother of two lovely little girls before she came of age. This left her free to come and go as she pleased, and since she pleased, during the early years of her marriage, to have me with her I was there as often as possible.

Although gay and pleasure loving, there was a serious side to her nature which was to develop with the years. Impulsively generous and kind, she could never see someone in trouble without trying to help. One night, just as I had gone to bed, I heard a noise downstairs and getting up saw Deborah in the hall in her filmy black nightdress and dressing gown trying to pacify a sobbing girl. Having settled her down at last on a couch on the landing Deborah took me into her bedroom and pointed out the window to the little public reserve opposite. 'I heard the girl screaming and saw her struggling with a man, so I went out and rescued her,' she said. She then rang the police and gave a description of the attacker.

Dr Hackett was dumbfounded to find a strange girl asleep on the landing when he came home, and perturbed when he heard that Deb had sent for the police, which might mean that his darling would have to appear in court. But this not worry Deb in the least. In fact she obviously enjoyed the drama of the situation when asked soon afterwards to identify the man from a police line-up. She told us that she recognised the fellow instantly but having cast him a look of utter disdain turned to the policeman and shook her head.

A sequel to this incident occurred some time later when Deb had become Lady Hackett. The Ladies' Guild to which she belonged was concerned at the time by a nest of rogues who were sending children out to beg and steal. The police had reported that two curly-haired little girls were frequently seen hanging around hotel doors but as they were quick and sly no one had yet succeeded in catching them.

Deb, walking home with a friend from a meeting of the Guild, saw two neglected looking children begging from passers-by.

'There they are,' Deb told her friend. 'You grab the little one.' Then, tossing aside her hat, handbag and parasol, she made off fleet as an emu after the older of the two imps. When the child climbed a fence Deb climbed too, falling over dustbins, rakes and spades in the yard of the Karrakatta Club, out into the Terrace and up to the corner of Milligan Street. Here the little girl darted down a lane, climbed a high stone wall at the end, and looking over her shoulder saw the huntress dropping over the wall like a cat. That wall, as it happened, led into the Hacketts' garden.

I was in at the kill when the small delinquent (the other child having made her escape) in the firm hands of a policeman was waiting the arrival of a Welfare officer. There she stood, a poor tousled frightened little wild thing, glaring in desperate defiance at Deb, who unable to bear anyone hating her, let alone a child, went and put her arms around her. 'No one's going to hurt you, dear. A kind man is coming soon to take you to a place where you will be loved and you'll grow up to be happy and good instead of naughty and miserable.'

The glare softened to a look of astonishment and the child burst into tears. 'If only I could grow up like you,' she wailed.

'You can,' said Deb, 'and I promise to help you.'

When the welfare officer, a quietly spoken, well set up young man, arrived at last he asked Deb whether she recognised him. She didn't, until he jogged her memory and then with a look of amusement and delight she held out her hand. He was the man in the line-up she had refrained from giving away to the police three years before. He told her that the incident had shaken him into deciding to give his life to good works. He had married the girl he had assaulted and they were now the parents of two children and had a happy home of their own.

Then there was the story of Fanny the parlourmaid. No one had noticed that she was in trouble and when she did not appear to wait on table at luncheon the housekeeper had told us that she had a cold. As Deb was off to open a bazaar and Dr Hackett to his office, they asked me, as a nurse, to have a look at the girl. The housekeeper, very prim in her black silk, then told me that she had dismissed Fanny without a reference because she was 'in the family way'. Where the girl had gone she didn't know or care, for she understood that the father of the child was a *married man*! She asked me, however, to call at the office and tell Dr Hackett, for this was not a subject she cared to discuss it with a gentleman and he must find some way to keep the shameful truth from his innocent young wife. This I did and as Deb scarcely knew the servants by name—apart from Nanny and the housekeeper—and was hardly likely to notice the appearance of a different parlourmaid, we decided to say nothing about it.

After dinner that night Deb started as usual thumping away on the piano and then suddenly she crashed down the lid and turned on me. 'You and John are keeping something from me. What is it?'

I had to tell her of course and she flounced off to bed in a rage, saying I had abused the laws of hospitality by sharing a secret with John.

I fled before breakfast for Deb had vowed she would never speak to me again, but when I met her in the Terrace a few days later she asked me to go home with her. In the meantime she had made it her business to find out where Fanny was taking refuge and had gone off alone to interview her. The end of it was that Fanny had her baby amidst loving care before going off with her little one to a new life on the goldfields.

Though beautiful, gracious and charming, Deb was also essentially practical and entirely individual in the way she acted and continued to act for the rest of her life.

Widowed at the age of twenty-nine, she married Frank Moulden in April 1918 and after his death in 1932 she married Basil Buller-Murphy. She was granted an Hon. Lit. D. by the University of Western Australia, was Chairman of Directors of Tantalite Ltd and Wolfram Industries, and director of various mining companies. As Mayoress of Adelaide she raised £100,000 for charitable causes and was the first passenger to fly to Europe.

She had tremendous talent and determination and could have been anything she chose, perhaps most of all—had that been her ambition—a great actress. She was to become undoubtedly one of the great women of Australia but to me she was always just Deb, the lovely, wild girl who galloped with me through the bush and told me of her love for the great man who was to set her feet on the path to fortune—and to fame.

7

Newspaper Work

✳ The shellbacked Tories,* as the conservatives were dubbed by the new order, were against the emancipation of women, considering that they should remain subject to their Tory-mindedness, get married and obey their husbands. But the Creator of the souls of men is not a Tory, and He has his own inexplicable ways of directing the affairs of men. Some call it the process of cause and effect. I call it the Hand on the Shoulder.

The Hand pushed me into the office of the *Morning Herald* in Perth where, to my amazement, the editor, John Leighton Nanson, M.P., offered me the position of social writer. He then handed me over to his wife, a charming, intellectual and joyous woman who had tired of doing this job herself but promised to help me.

She came in every afternoon for tea which we made over a spirit lamp, and drank with lemon instead of milk. She brought her friends and gave cheerful advice, telling me not to mind my hopeless spelling and handwriting as the editor would deal with it. She had read some of my stories and knew I could write and that I knew everyone socially, which was all that mattered.

I also had the help and advice of my friend Muriel Chase who wrote social notes for *The West Australian* under the pen-name of 'Adrienne'. Muriel was a darling, younger by about five years than myself, beautiful and serene and though born and bred in what outsiders called 'the land of sin, sorrow and sandy blight', cultured and widely read. We were vaguely connected—as who among the

* *Shellbacked Tories*: The use of this term is an interesting indication of the divergence between Western Australia and the other States, where the term 'shellback' denoted a person of convict origin whose back was liable to be hardened by the effects of the lash. In Western Australia the term retained the British interpretation as one of slow-moving, conservative habits reminiscent of the tortoise or the snail.

descendants of those early settlers were not?—her great-grandfather having been that same Marshall Waller Clifton of Australind whose grandson Robert Cecil had married my Aunt Blanche. Perhaps it was of some significance that she was also connected, through Marshall Waller's wife, with the great pioneer of prison reform, Elizabeth Fry. Muriel was a reformer born and in her gentle, unobtrusive way did more for the social welfare of her State than can ever be known.

In 1901, when just twenty years old, she was married—socially well, financially poorly but undoubtedly for love—to Ernest Chase. They had spent the first year of their married life in England, but the climate soon drove them back to Western Australia where Ernest became aide-de-camp and private secretary to the Governor.

Towards the end of 1902 Sir Winthrop Hackett had offered Muriel a position on his two papers, *The West Australian* and the weekly *The Western Mail*. Mrs Nanson, from whom I took over on *The Morning Herald* in the following year, had previously been social editress to these papers and had also started a children's section in *The Western Mail* under the name of Aunt Mary. Muriel therefore undertook not only the social notes but the role of aunt to the thousands of young Western Australians who, under her inspired guidance, helped with the establishment of the Silver Chain Nursing Association for the care of the aged. She was to continue in this work for thirty-four years, and over that time, although I had long since abandoned all thought of a journalistic career, our friendship was to continue unimpaired.

The West Australian, edited by Winthrop Hackett, was the leading newspaper in the State but although I knew Dr Hackett very well indeed he had refused to take my writing seriously. I had once submitted to him an article entitled 'Going to the Royal Show', a conscientious effort on my part that had caused him considerable amusement. He had then looked at me in his visionary way, handed back my script and indicated that journalism was not for me.

But here I was, in at the office in the morning, often not back home until after midnight. My beaux would bring me back to the *Herald* office from parties and dances, munching sandwiches snaffled from tables before the supper room had opened, leaving me with laughter and teasing jokes. I would then find my way to the sub-editor's den, write my report and hand over the ill-spelt, ill-written, inky pages.

Poor Mr Lambert*—God rest his soul!—must have hated editing such a scrawl. The only indication of his feelings was his silence broken by an occasional groan. He was always very kind to me, almost tender, as though aware not only of my inexperience, which was obvious, but of my trembling humility and pathetic pride.

I sat in his office at night, for the reporters of that time were a rough and ready crowd, boisterous and inclined to be fresh after handing in their news of crime, disasters and sudden deaths. But, taken all in all, men were more respectful and considerate of women in those days and we had nothing to fear. Muriel Chase, who was by any standard lovely to look at, went around highways and byways alone and was treated everywhere like royalty. And so, in fact, was I.

It was all I could do to keep up appearances on the two pounds a week salary I earned but I was enjoying myself. Weddings were really my only bane. Whether Church of England, Roman Catholic, Congregational, Wesleyan or Jewish they were all the same—the blushing bride, the nervous bridegroom, the triumphant parents. Weddings roused my utmost contempt. Why all this musical comedy pretence, I wondered, when so few marriages proved abiding and true?

Between rushes I wrote articles for the *Herald* which, though unsigned and unpaid for, were a means of exercising the craft I felt tingling in my fingers. I wrote up all the charitable organisations then coming into being with our growing prosperity. There were orphanages; institutions for the blind, deaf and dumb; an industrial school for boys of 'the lower order'; and the Home of the Good Shepherd run by the Sisters of Mercy for 'fallen girls'. How I grew to love these nuns with their Irish humour that sparkled when they told me of the delinquent girls and women they were working Old Sin out of in the laundry.

I was seeing life at last, watching it with my one part visual sight and three parts 'blindman's sense' of touch, colour, shape, form, hearing, smell, taste, intuition and impression. Working on a paper had the advantage of keeping me in touch with everything that was going on. Labor was gathering power to strike. Prosperity was bounding in spite of new premiers in and out of office like jack-in-the-boxes.

* Herbert James Lambert, born South Australia 1876, joined *Morning Herald* (Perth) 1899, *The West Australian* in 1920, and became editor in 1929. Columns he conducted under pen-names of 'Scrutator' and 'The Walrus' were a vehicle for his gentle and humorous philosophy. He died in 1958.

The population of the State had risen from 65,000 ten years before to 190,000. The foundation of the new Law Courts was laid and building was in progress. The Teachers' Training College was opened at Claremont.

Disasters too! Fifty thousand pounds gone up in smoke at Fremantle—fires on steamers, at the Vacuum Oil Company and the warehouse of Harris, Scarfe and Sandovers. Another at number 1 timber mill in the south-west. Terrible storms and loss of ships in the Bight but then no alternative means of travelling to the other States. New lighthouses built and memorials unveiled. An outbreak of bubonic plague and a yellow flag flying over a residence in Hill Street where a victim had died, and everyone avoiding the locality. Dr Black of the Health Department escorted me into his back yard to look at the rats he kept in wooden cages so that he could study 'how the fleas jumped'.

I wrote an article on enteric fever which brought doctors in to ask the author's identity. Mr Nanson, knowing I had no medical standing beyond a despised nurse's certificate, hesitated to tell them but they persisted and he finally confessed. That was the end of it, for although the doctors admitted that the article had merit they declared it a danger to the public for anyone outside the profession to write on medical topics.

'But wait a minute,' Mr Nanson said, taking pity on my crest-fallen face. 'The Church of England has paid us to reprint your article on the Parkerville Orphans' Home and send it round, in loose leaf, with Saturday morning's paper. They've already had subscriptions and donations of goods as a result of it, so don't lose heart.'

That cheered me up and I began writing articles for *The West Australian* under the nom-de-plume of Echo. I owed this chance largely to the help of Alfred Carson who was then associate editor to Dr Hackett on *The West Australian* and editor of *The Western Mail*. A little man with a big heart, Mr Carson was the son of the first mechanical engineer to come to the colony—a man of whose achievements his descendants were justly proud. It was this earlier Alfred Carson who had made the printing machine for the pioneer newspaper *The Perth Gazette*. He had later installed the Town Hall clock, made the weather cock for Wesley Church and had studied acoustics when this science was unheard of in the colony. But most remarkable of all he had extracted an inflammable gas from blackboy trees which he stored in bullock bladders and used in his own home.

Mr Carson would talk of his grandfather's exploits by the hour, though of his own achievements he was extremely modest. Among the many good causes he espoused was The Silver Chain, in the early development of which he was closely associated with Muriel Chase. Perhaps he saw me as a good cause too for he warmly encouraged my idea of writing a series of sketches called 'Adventures of a Nurse in Australia'. These—after I suppose a certain amount of editorial doctoring—he put on the front page and saw that I was paid well for them.

He promised to guard my identity and I had great fun. My most faithful swain at that time was a surveyor who was always suggesting that I should give up writing social notes and open a nursing home in the agricultural area where he was working. 'After all,' he said, 'it's not as if you could write real stuff, like Echo.'

But the real stuff soon came to an end. Mrs Edith Cowan, a determined and spirited social welfare worker and destined to be the first woman M.P. in Australia, was at this time fighting for an up-to-date maternity hospital in Perth—an ambition later realised in the establishment of the King Edward Memorial Hospital. Fired by one of my articles called 'Midwifery on the Fields', she approached Mr Carson, demanding the identity of the writer. Mr Carson kept his promise to me, but Mrs Cowan insisted that anyone who could write with such understanding of the question was too valuable to be ignored. Mr Carson took me out to lunch to explain the situation and I gave in. And that was an end of that because once the cat was out of the bag those articles were known to have been fictional and were therefore considered quite valueless.

I felt I couldn't go on merely describing the social doings of the town, but in any case, while I was still debating the matter, the *Morning Herald* was sold to the Roman Catholic Church for their weekly *The Record* on which they did not need a lady reporter.

What to do now? To marry and have children? The thought often occupied my mind. Chances had come my way, if never the gallant hero of my romantic dreams. As time went on, however, I became resigned to the idea that I was not meant to find fulfilment in marriage because of the risk of passing on my physical defects. I had been deprived of the two things I had most desired—love and the opportunity to write. To say it did not hurt would be untrue. It would be untrue also to say that I was sure at this time of being pushed by the Hand of God. Although I never lost a sense of that Presence that had come to me as a child, I was neither virtuous nor pious and sometimes my harp strings produced the sharp notes of jealousy and bickering—especially with my sisters. Though blessed with the gifts of faith and hope, I still knew little of charity. I did not know that charity is love in its sublimest form and that its roots lie in one's own power of giving love. I was still sure, however, that I would not have been born had there not been something I was meant to do in life and that I must go on looking for it.

Newspaper work had developed my confidence, and opposition had strengthened my independence, but though I wanted nothing more than to write, it was clear that I must relinquish this urge for a time at least. I was still in my twenties and I had already, with little education or training in the craft, won prizes for my writing and the Devil himself couldn't take that from me.

After trying private nursing once in the country, once in the suburbs and once in a camp at Canning Bridge I was sickened of it. In those days a nurse was supposed never to sleep, to do most of the housework and cooking, never to go off duty or to read to herself. One was expected to entertain the husband when he came home, to amuse the children, mind the baby, and give oneself, body and soul, into the fretful keeping of one's patient.

I once heard my Uncle Harry say to Dr Athelston Saw: 'I can't get a nurse for love nor money', to which the other replied: 'I can never get one for love, but I can for money.' My uncle then asked me to relieve the nurse who had become exhausted looking after an enteric fever case who was the doctor in charge of the Lunatic Asylum, but I was informed that since the patient was 'in the profession' I could expect only half fees. I wanted to refuse but I went—perhaps for love.

This young doctor and his colleagues had promised each other to try out a new treatment if any of them got enteric and it had fallen to his lot to be the guinea pig. With the help of several doctors and nurses he was lowered, each day, into a bath of ice water which caused him to suffer excruciating muscular pains and made him indescribably irritable. As his strength had to be maintained with hourly spoonsful of nourishment I had to remain awake all night, so I sat up behind the screened foot of his bed, reading by the light of a candle. At the end of a week he ordered me to fetch his other nurse, saying he could not stand the sight of a new shadow a minute longer. Now exhausted myself from lack of sleep and constant abuse, I walked out of the house and although he sent a message for me to come back I had by that time made other plans.

I loved the country and felt now that I must be meant to go out and help those who were struggling to develop it. I had no fear of losing anything by so doing for I had nothing to lose. In fact, I had little fear of a physical nature. Since seeing my father die I was less afraid of death, but I was afraid of shadows, of unseen presences, inexplicable noises in the night, and of infuriated animals. Poverty and hardship, however, though I would have preferred not to embrace them, I knew could not kill me. People in high places could not intimidate me, though I wanted them to like me. I still had a sickening fear of facing another's anger, but I had uncanny power over the mentally deranged and was soon to find that I could calm the most demented cases of delirium tremens.

Life is like the old rhyme: 'The fire began to burn the stick, the stick began to beat the dog . . .' I answered a call for help from the M.O. in Wagin, 193 miles by rail from Perth. I liked the place and its doctor, who suggested that I should take a house there and help him with his cases.

And so it was that the fire began to burn the stick, the stick began to beat the dog, the dog began to bite the pig and the stupid little pig jumped over the stile. In other words, I got hold of some beds and furnishings and started up a nursing home in that little country town.

8

Wagin

The original pioneers of the Wagin district, a small but sturdy band, had been helped in their battle against the virgin bush by indentured servants and ticket-of-leave men. Later the settlers of this district had the assistance of wholesome and industrious German immigrants, driven from their country by political disturbances. They worked without complaint and minded their own business.

In the early years of settlement the farmers had taken their bullock wagons for more than a hundred miles over rough bush tracks to Albany to collect their stores, for up to that time the railway did not extend south of Beverley.

During the decade preceding my arrival, however, the country which had previously been used for open range grazing had been found suitable for growing cereals and fruit and (except in areas containing a poison plant) for cattle raising. Since then the population of 170 people had increased by 1000 and the railway line had been extended to Albany. Many of the newcomers were people from the goldfields anxious to exploit the possibilities of the more congenial south-west. Every train brought more arrivals, mostly ex-diggers and their families with all their worldly goods who would drive off to new locations in the wilderness. The store was doing good business, the wheelwright continually building sulkies and carts, the horse dealer bringing in horses, the blacksmith working after hours, the two hotels often packed out. The boarding-house run by the genteel Misses Wright was overflowing, and the postmaster was demented trying to sort out names and addresses. A letter might be addressed

> Harry or Ikey Smith,
> Taken up land by a lake,
> Dumbell or some such (meaning Dumbleyung),
> Wagin

or

Jim Robinson,
Candlelight

or

Ned Jones,
Wishbone

or

Mr Tom Tucker,
Kukerin

all places within fifty miles eastward. And believe me these letters
would reach their destination.

The tracks leading out in every direction were full of holes, and
obstructed by roots and fallen trees, so every cart carried an axe. Like
the spokes of a wheel were these tracks from the settlement to the
scattered holdings and farms, and to the camps of the timber-getters,
sleeper-cutters, shepherds, and gatherers of mallee bark for tanning
purposes.

But except for the bushmen who came to me with mallee poisoned
hands, it was the people in and around the township who were my
main concern. These were mostly sterling farmers who had made
good, but there were a few reprobates among them, like the old man
who had built himself a fine house but insisted on living under it
with his native woman and their children. This scandalised the people
of Wagin who set a high standard of respectability. If a girl got into
trouble the boy responsible had to marry her.

Protestant bodies held regular services in the Hall. The Anglicans
were ministered to by the Rev. Atwell and his wife, while a lone
priest shepherded the Roman Catholic flock from Albany to Beverley.
When anyone died there was a proper funeral. The carpenter would
polish and embellish the coffin, and the black horse would be taken
out of the baker's cart and harnessed to the glass hearse kept in the
carpenter's barn.

The police sergeant went about in cloth uniform with silver
buttons on the hottest day and once a month the Court was conducted with dignity and decorum by Dr House from Katanning, the
accused sometimes being allowed to go home on remand to milk his
cows or get on with his fencing.

The house I secured was at the back of the town dam, and was
built solidly of stone. It had six rooms and several 'cubbies' on the
verandah, plus a separate tumbledown brick kitchen with a room

attached. When Mrs Jones, our old general at Applecross, saddled herself with a mysterious girl of eight it suited Mother to pass them both on to me, but I was glad enough to have help in that little brick shack. 'Em,' Mrs Jones would say to the stray child, 'if yer don't be'ave I'll send yer back ter the Collie 'Ome.' Other help I secured now and then—a farmer's sister, or widow of uncertain age, who slept in one 'cubby', I in another. The front rooms were transformed into wards, those at the back into surgery and sitting-rooms.

Patients did not come quickly nor joyfully, but they came in sufficient numbers to cover overhead expenses. I was independent at last, and happy in this pocket handkerchief of a place in a corner of the bush—a handkerchief twisted and soiled with grime and tears but that shared the pocket with lovely things like hope and courage.

Here I found balm for my troubled spirit in the love I saw in the eyes of sick bush children, in the clasp of hands when I had been able to relieve pain, in the touching gratitude of people for whom I had merely carried out my obvious duty. I found it in little gifts of flowers, butter, eggs and cakes left at my door, and I began to grow new and sturdier feathers in place of the golden ones that had been plucked from me.

Gone these thirty years or more is Dr George Edward Vere de Vere St. John Quinton, and forgotten by most, but by myself, not as long as I live. I had liked him from the time of our first meeting, during my previous visit to Wagin, and he remained my friend to the end of his life, though many wondered how I managed to put up with him, let alone defend him. I see him as though it were yesterday, standing there in the sitting room of my Wagin nursing home, in his top boots and leather breeches, his cutaway coat and waistcoat, his great stock tie with the horseshoe on it, his magnificent head thrown back in defiance.

Not long after my arrival he had had a case of whisky sent to me and when I explained to him that I never touched the stuff he replied: 'But I do, be gad.' And didn't he just! When he had looked at his patients he would demand that I brought out a bottle and after a drink or two would start in on the stories of his ill-spent life 'They're all barbarians in this damned place,' he would declare, 'but you've at least seen the world I come from. You understand *something* about it. The rest of them know nothing at all.' Then out would roll his memories of hunting and horses, of cards, dice, and debts, of women and wine.

Born of the British aristocracy and the cousin of a duke, educated at Harrow and Oxford and later an officer in the Guards, his wild spirits had led him into trouble and he had been shipped out to Australia to make good. On arrival in Melbourne he had joined the mounted police in which he had helped to eradicate the last of the Australian bushrangers. These were not the brave and sometimes even gallant men driven to lawless living by cruel conditions in the convict gangs or the injustices of the gold rush period, but a later crop who hid behind the skirts of their womenfolk or other relatives. Many of the conditions he dealt with had come as a result of the passing of the Robertson Act which aimed to divide the vast holdings of the squatters among the land-hungry newcomers. Naturally enough, the squatters, resentful at having what they now considered as their 'birthright' filched from them, frequently offered bribes to small men—with no real wish to work the land anyway—to act as 'dummies' on small holdings officially held in their names. Truly is it said that 'the Devil finds work for idle hands' and the shacks of these dummy holders were often the centres of petty crime, sheltering horse thieves or 'moonlighters' who rode out at night mustering stock on surrounding properties and selling it to unscrupulous butchers or so-called 'fiddlers' who acted as go-betweens.

When in Melbourne Police Trooper George Edward Vere de Vere St. John Quinton rode in steeplechases and dined at Government House where he met an aristocratic English beauty whom he vowed, at first sight, to make his wife. But however noble his lineage Quinton —mounted or not—was a policeman and as such quite unacceptable to a lady of this standing. So he went back to England, graduated in medicine, returned and married her. For a man of his type to have shown such persistence indicates that he must have loved this woman deeply. What went wrong I could never really make out. Sometimes he would pause in his narration and raise his glass. 'William, sweet William,' he would murmur, 'my son, my son.' Once, after telling me of having left his wife, I remarked casually: 'But I expect you'll see her again.' He looked at me savagely and pointing to the floor said: 'If she were standing *there* I would not see her!'

Strangely, the people of Wagin were proud of their aristocratic resident doctor, admired his lordly ways and were enchanted by his appearance at local functions dressed like a duke in full evening dress. His carryings-on gave them an endless topic of conversation, but because of his unpredictable behaviour and his tendency to abuse his patients they also feared him.

He was a good doctor and an excellent surgeon and did not spare himself in administering to the sick. He taught me many things, among them defiance in the face of unjust criticism and the courage to be oneself, though his arrogance, eccentricity and egotism often roused me to nauseating rage. He quite frequently humiliated me—or tried to—to protect his own overweening pride and finally with a gross injustice that put an end to our association.

He liked nothing better than to show off his horsey clothes, his fine appearance on a good mount and his stylish horsemanship. I procured a hollow-backed filly and a secondhand side-saddle, and in my long skirt, blouse and straw hat could jump after him over logs and gallop past him in the scrub. That upset his dignity and he would roar at me all the way home about my poor seat in the saddle and my abomination of an old moke. I soon tired of that and made excuses whenever the matter of riding excursions was raised.

One day thereafter he arrived at my front door with a four-horse-drawn wagonette filled with all the barmaids and barmen he could muster. He told me that he had organised a picnic in my honour at the top of the Wagin hill and they had brought plenty of good things to eat and drink—alcoholic and otherwise. At the height of the proceedings Quinton stood on the brow of the hill and indicating the plain beneath, said: 'All these things shall be thine, if thou wilt worship me.' I was scandalised and not a little frightened by what I considered his blasphemy, but little he cared whose feelings he upset.

One evening he dashed up to the gate, holding between the shafts a stamping, snorting chestnut.

'Bring my bag,' he yelled, 'and hop in. I can't hold this brute much longer.'

Throwing the bag in, I scrambled after it and we bolted off down the track, through a patch of scrub and out on to the highway, where I breathed more easily.

'Belongs to the publican,' Quinton explained. 'Satan by name and Satan by nature. No one else would break him in, so I undertook the job myself.'

A queer way to break in a horse, I thought—putting it straight into a sulky and expecting a nurse to share the fun. But that wasn't the full story. 'Urgent call from a cocky farmer,' he added. 'His missus was gored by a cow and she's had her baby in the cowshed. No time to get hold of a decent nag.'

He then produced his hunting horn which, along with his gold-mounted riding crop, was the joy of his life, and blew a resounding blast. I was petrified. If the reins (twisted round both his hands) had broken, if the horse had lost its footing on the rough road, if a roo or a rabbit had crossed our path, it would have been all up with us. But there must have been a galling bit in that foaming mouth for Satan began to slacken pace and settled at last into a trot. This, however, did not suit Quinton's mood. As we approached a paddock near the steep Wagin hill he noticed some Chinese workers burning off.

'Watch me put the fear of hell into those Chinks,' he yelled and putting the horn to his lips blasted it again.

The Chinese, more entertained than alarmed, waved, jumped about and threw burning sticks into the air as the frenzied Satan took that mile long hill at a gallop and plunged down the other side at the speed of sound. It was more even than Quinton himself had bargained for. 'God save us!' he bellowed and yelled a repeated warning as we hurtled on: 'If there's anything on the road, *get out of the way*!'

If there was, they must have gone, for we got to our destination without mishap. Two men ran out and grabbed Satan's lathered bit on either side and we alighted—I at least with trembling knees.

It's hard to believe that anyone who could behave so irresponsibly with an unbroken horse could, all in a moment, become the gentle and responsible physician. The patient had been carried into a miser-able, dark kitchen and put on to a bed. She was moaning pitifully, not so much because of her wound, but because she had lost her baby. Quinton wiped her tears with his huge, blue handkerchief and told her not to grieve as she could make another baby as soon as she liked after he had fixed her up. He gave her morphia, called for a whisky for himself and signed to me to set out the sterilised instruments and a towel from his bag. He then called for a clean saucepan but as the only one they had was full of stew they fetched a frying pan.

The family dismissed, he helped me undress the patient, talking the while like a mother to a hurt child. He cleaned the gaping wound in her side with carbolic diluted in a milk bowl and while I administered chloroform, snipped forceps on the torn blood vessels, tied them with sterilised catgut from a bottle, and stitched the wound with horsehair he had boiled in the frying pan. He then told me to carry on while he got the sulky ready for the return drive.

As the men let go the horse's head we shot through the gate like a rocket, but Satan evidently preferred the doctor's hold on the reins to the rough hands of the agitated farmers on its bit and snaffle. We proceeded steadily home, Quinton singing all the way: 'When I am dead, my dearest, strew on me roses, roses . . .'

I realised that this man was actually a wizard with horses and loved them with all his heart. He had bought for a song a miserable, piebald cob which he fed back to health on oats and mash, and groomed himself, blackening its hooves, cropping its mane, docking its tail and polishing a saddle for its back. Not long afterwards it won a blue ribbon at the Royal Show and he sold it as a gentleman's hack for £50.

Another time he sent for me to sit beside the sick wife of the proprietor of the Commercial Travellers' Hotel. When I arrived he said: 'I've done my damnedest—she'll either die in the night or get over it. I'll be on the couch outside if you need me.'

The patient, a pleasing, well-liked woman, was deeply drugged and there was nothing to do. Trying to keep awake all night in a firelit room is agony, and at some stage I dozed. Starting awake towards dawn I cast one glance towards the sick woman, who lay so white and still that I thought she was dead. I called the doctor and he came staggering in from his whisky-soaked dreams, blinked at me, muttered and stumped out again. Automatically I went to refill the patient's hot water bottles and found to my astonishment that she was quite warm, her pulse and respiration normal. I felt more than a fool at having called the doctor but before I could go after him to say that all was well, into the room trooped a tousled procession of hotel guests, including a commercial traveller and a visiting dentist, closely followed by the doctor and the distraught husband who threw himself on his knees beside the bed.

Quinton shook his fist at the other men, asking in a stage whisper what the hell they were doing there, whereupon it was found that he had gone from room to room in search of the husband, calling out at each door that he must come at once, and each had thought he was wanted urgently.

It was at this stage that the patient yawned, opened her eyes and smiled placidly at everyone, then put her hand out and rubbed her husband's hair. Quinton began to laugh. 'I said she'd be dead or better,' he roared, 'and as you see, she's not dead.' At that everyone, including the patient, joined in the joke and the publican got to his feet and led the way to the bar.

But Quinton was not always so amiable. I called him once to a woman who had been brought to my hospital with septicaemia and in a desperate condition. Quinton spared himself no pains to save her life but he cursed and swore at her for having brought the trouble on herself by having failed to consult him earlier. She was a bold, handsome wench, even when so sick, and her husband—we'll call him Pat O'Grady—a bold, handsome fellow, a foreman on the railways, was a local leader of the new Labor movement. Anxious about his wife, he came every day, chopped wood and kept the kitchen fire alight for boiling the water Quinton used when treating her.

Her condition was still critical some days later when Quinton rode up on his piebald which he had just taken over a barbed wire fence. The horse was badly cut and he shouted to me to bring a bucket of hot water and a pot of ointment so that he could dress the wound.

'The hot water's for my missus,' Pat said. 'I'll boil you up some more for your horse when you've seen to her.'

The doctor straightened up and looking like a bull about to charge, rolled up his shirt sleeves. 'Pat O'Grady,' he said, 'I see you wish me to show you who's who in this town. All right—put 'em up.'

Pat shook his head. 'Y' oughta be ashamed of yourself,' he said, 'picking a brawl, with a woman dying inside there.'

'So you're yellow, eh?' Quinton taunted him.

Pat flushed but controlled himself admirably. 'I'd not fight an old man,' he said. 'I'd floor ye in the first round.'

Quinton, superbly arrogant, continued to challenge him and Pat had begun to remove his coat when we were all suddenly petrified by screams from the window of my front ward. Pat was off like a shot, I after him, while Quinton turned to tend his horse. When I reached the ward I found Pat holding his wife in his arms.

'I'll not have you fight that brute, Pat,' she sobbed. 'He'd murder you.'

The scene brought me to my nursing senses. I helped Pat put the patient back to bed and sent him away. I expected her to be in a state of collapse but instead she was charged with the energy of anger. 'I'll not see that doctor again so long as I live. I'll die before I let him put a finger on me again.'

She was still carrying on when Quinton appeared in the doorway, brandishing his riding whip. 'This is what you need, my beauty,' he said, 'but being your doctor I have to get you better first.'

'Get out of my sight,' the woman raged. 'I've done with you, do you hear, and I'll be outa this place tomorrow.'

Marvel of marvels she was—and walking on her two feet. Getting out of bed in a rage, which we thought would have been the death of her, had apparently brought about her cure.

Although the townspeople of Wagin continued to be proud of their doctor and even to boast of him, more and more began going to Katanning or even Perth to be treated for their complaints or to have their babies. The cases in my hospital declined to a few emergencies or casualties such as broken limbs or poisoned hands.

Dr House of Katanning had often asked me to open a nursing home there for him as there was as yet no hospital in that centre. I had hesitated, not wanting to desert Wagin and its eccentric, infuriating but somehow likeable medico. In the end Dr Quinton made up my mind for me by blaming me for the loss of a mother and her premature baby—a complicated case in which he had arrived too late to assist. Though burning with indignation at the time, I soon managed to forgive him and remained his friend.

During the next ten years he moved from town to town, leaving behind him in each a dubious reputation and a fund of anecdotes. He often sent me boxes of fruit and flowers and occasionally a despairing note: 'Sister Skinner! Sister Skinner, come to me! Come and help me out in this hell of a place I'm in.' But I did not go.

By coincidence I happened to be acting as night superintendent at the large hospital to which he was brought to die. He had a special attendant, for he was heavy to handle and as the cousin of a duke and a long-standing officer of the Medical Department, he was an important person.

Though more cantankerous than ever he retained to the end his power of enchantment over all and sundry. He demanded flowers for his room, fruit and champagne for his visitors and would insist on being dressed each morning in his hunting coat, white stock tie and velvet cap. Then he would be moved into a chair by the window where he would shout jibes about how badly we treated horses in this benighted country. In the evenings he insisted on being brushed, shaved and groomed as if for a levee and would entertain everyone who came into his room, even probationers and wardsmaids, with scandalous stories of the Royal Family and the immoral behaviour of his aristocratic relatives.

Often in the night watches he would yell for me and shout abuse at his male nurse and all the others who assisted him. One day a Madonna-faced senior sister came to me, very embarrassed, and said: 'Dr Quinton's carrying on very badly again. He says he won't stop unless you come and kiss him goodnight.'

When I came in he grinned at me in his cockeyed mischievous way and held out his trembling hands. There stood the Matron in her dressing gown, evidently roused from her sleep by his yelling.

'She won't kiss me now, Matron,' he complained, insinuating, to disconcert me, that I had not hesitated to do so previously.

To my surprise, the Matron, whom I had thought so severe, woke up to his little game. She pushed the younger nurse forward, whispering, '*You* kiss him, Sister.' The girl did so, gently and sweetly on his clammy brow and he was satisfied.

A few days later when I came in to him he raised a feeble hand in greeting and asked for his horn and crop and the silver cup he had won in a Melbourne steeplechase. We put them in his hands and he called as loudly as he could: 'Halloo! Gone away! Gone away!' Then with a contented smile he slipped off to ride with the Four Horsemen of the Apocalypse.

9

Katanning

Katanning, the centre of the South-Western Division, was only a little over thirty miles from Wagin, but much more advanced. When I came there in 1906 it boasted a flour mill, a newspaper, a courthouse, a road board and a government land agency office which organised the settlement of the three million acres of unimproved bushlands of the area then open for selection.

Its leading people were of the old order which held fast to the traditions of the Crown colony. Mr F. H. Piesse, M.P., was the king-pin, Kobeelya, his grand house on the hill (now a girls' college) being evidence of his importance. Other well-to-do families lived on outlying properties mostly on the west side which area had been taken up early on by moneyed folk. The social stratas in this division were very pronounced and since I had let the side down by being a nurse, I was socially more or less out of the upper layer.

The only house I could procure was a mean one, its main assets a good operating table and a glass-fronted instrument cupboard.

I was fortunate, however, in finding a good friend in Dr F. M. House, who had come out from England in 1892, practised for a while in Beverley and Katanning and then in the north-west port of Derby for four years. He had thereafter returned to Beverley but much of his heart remained in the wild northern region and in 1901 he had gone there once again, this time as doctor and naturalist to a party led by Surveyor Fred Drake-Brockman, the father of my friend Deb Hackett. The purpose of this expedition had been to explore the last extensive area of unmapped land in Australia—a rugged triangle of country in north-western Kimberley.

When going around the country together to visit patients, I never tired of hearing of his experiences in this trackless land, nor he of relating them. He conjured up for me vivid pictures of the vast, empty savannahs of the Kimberleys, the rough, impenetrable ranges, mighty, crocodile-infested rivers and lily-covered billabongs. I loved to hear of the giant tides and cyclones of that adventurous coast and of the pearling industry that had brought to it a fascinating and polyglot population.

Particularly interested in trees, he told me of the huge, bottle-shaped baobabs—ungainly parents of beautiful, creamy blossoms, of the graceful bauhenias with their honey-sweet pink flowers and long beans that shone crimson in the sun, of the dazzling yellow flowers of the wild cotton trees, of the stately kurrajongs, ragged coolibahs and cadjiputs, the gleaming trunks of the white gums, the sweet-smelling sandalwood and pituri.

Exciting, too, it was to hear of their encounters with wild Aborigines, who had viewed them with guarded curiosity but allowed them to pass unmolested. On one occasion only had he been non-plussed by them, and that was when he had been asked to pit his skill as a medicine man against a tribal dignitary of that reputation. Could he 'sing rain'? He had gazed hopefully into the sky, where there was not a sign of a cloud, gestured and sung a hymn or two. Before long, sure enough clouds began to bank up, and that night, all out of season, it rained a few points. His reputation as a sorcerer was established beyond doubt and his Aboriginal counterpart was the first to congratulate him.

He had been tremendously impressed with the indomitable spirit and courage of the Kimberley pioneers and also with their unfailing good humour. They made light of everything, he told me, one of them even of having his leg amputated on a wharf, without anaesthetic.

Dr House told me of his adventures because I pressed him to do so and he knew they delighted me, though many people of the district knew nothing of this colourful episode in the life of their reserved and respected doctor and magistrate. Normally he preferred to leave others to do the talking, listening to their stories with quiet understanding, helping and advising friends and patients when he could and loving them as a shepherd loves his sheep.

Many of the bushmen I encountered in the south-west were of similar calibre and toughness to those Dr House had met in the north. I was filled with admiration of their courage and courtesy though some were very rough diamonds indeed—and how they hated to be nursed! ''Ere blimey,' they would say, 'yer don't need ter wash me. I'm clean aren't I?' They were quite indifferent to fancy food, all they wanted being cold mutton and pickles, washed down with strong black tea. And how grateful they were, stammering their awkward thanks as they went on their way.

A cocky farmer named Joe Strut was brought in one day with both legs and one arm broken. I couldn't get him to part with his shirt (we discovered later that he kept his money sewn inside it); the most he would allow me to do being to cut off the sleeve. His trousers were made of undressed leather and to my amazement stood up on their own when thrown aside. He was some weeks recovering and on returning home he sent me the following letter which I have cherished ever since:

Dere Nurse,

I has a house, 2 springing heifers, 2 cows and a bull, 5 acres under crop, 14 cleared waitin burning off, 1 fenced with pigs, 10 sheep and ram, me old Ma what wants lookin arter. Are you willin? I had a good education like you as.

Yr faithful
Joe Strut

Staff was a problem in my little hospital but I solved it to some extent by enlisting the help of my sister Mittie, hiring local folk for extra work and getting a nurse from Perth when necessary. Dear little Mittie was fairly capable and industrious when it pleased her. I could trust her to do what she considered her duty. If no one was very ill I could leave her in charge of the hospital when attending outside cases with Dr House, though I never knew what would be the result and always returned in some trepidation. She was pretty, full of humour and with a quickness of tongue that was often disconcerting but she did not take kindly to instructions from her sister. At the slightest hint of rebuke she would run off to shelter with Mrs House, to whom she had become attached soon after her arrival. Mittie did not take kindly to being ignored, along with my hospital, by the Upper Ten but being Mrs House's friend gave her entrée to local society.

We were given a turkey for Christmas and as we had an unusual number of patients Mittie decided to make a specially rich plum pudding. When taking the turkey from the oven she dropped the baking dish and in a temperature of 101 degrees we had to mop up a sea of grease, then when the pudding was fished out of the pot it looked like a deflated football and turned out like a plate of parrot food. Mittie had forgotten to add the suet.

I looked at her, my face pouring with sweat, my white uniform spotted with grease. 'Oh Mittie!' I said. Nothing more, but that was enough. She just flounced off to share the Houses' Christmas spread.

She made no apologies but she did try to make up, offering, soon afterwards, to take over everything else while I concentrated on a 'middy' case that was really one person's work. She was as good as gold, seeing to all the other patients and preparing the meals.

One night when I came off duty, a new baby in its cradle, the mother resting peacefully and I worn out, I found Mittie with her feet up reading in the sitting room, washing-up piled high in the sink, the kitchen chaotic. 'Oh, Mittie!' I said. She threw the book aside and stamped out the back door—the nearest way to the Houses' bungalow. I could have cried. Then I heard a yell and a commotion in the yard that set me running to investigate. Mittie in her proud dignity had fallen over the reclining cow and gone head first into the manure heap. I laughed till I was nearly sick and Mittie laughed too and all else was forgotten.

For all her failings dear Mittie was a great help to me, while she lasted. She would hunt depression from the wards with her capers, painting her face and playing the fool, mimicking, mincing, jigging and singing popular music hall numbers of the day—'The Boy I Love Is Up in the Gallery', 'Daisy, Daisy'—and grand opera too, 'Toreador,' 'The Barber of Seville' . . .

It was not long, however, before she tired of putting up with me and my dreary job and went home to Mother and her bright young friends. Mittie never married, though she had chances enough. I think she couldn't bear the thought of leaving Mother, and when Mother died she sacrificed her life to Jack.

After Mittie left me Julie turned up with her two children, and the tempo of life quickened considerably. Julie was kith of my father, a descendant on the distaff side of Louis XVI whose portrait she resembled strikingly. Although not technically beautiful she had one of the most fascinating personalities I have ever encountered and she had only to look at a man with her flashing green eyes to have him at her feet. Always a wilful and spirited girl, she had run away from her English home at seventeen to marry a man who brought her out to the goldfields. Now she had come to me because of a row with her husband over someone called Percy, a rich young man who had been paying her attention since they left the fields.

'My relationship with Percy is purely platonic,' Julie insisted, 'but Charlie's so jealous. He goes off to work all day, leaving me alone with the kids. Why shouldn't we go out in Percy's yacht? I mean— can you blame me?'

I couldn't blame her for anything. To me she was just the Julie I had loved when we were children together in England, someone to whom I could talk without reservation. She more or less did what she liked with me.

Her charm soon became a byword in the district and she was invited everywhere, but unlike Mittie she refused to go anywhere without me. If I was unable to go she turned the invitation down, no matter how interesting the occasion promised to be. Therefore, whenever I had a nurse to leave in charge Julie and I would sally forth together and I met 'the best people' at last. I saw a lot of the surrounding district in this way, sometimes staying at outlying properties overnight to rest the horses that were a very important consideration in those days. What splendid animals they were too— bloodstock with pedigrees as long as the members of a royal house and the pride of their respective owners.

Julie's being often out, however, did not prevent young men from haunting the hospital, making free with my larder and sitting-room and staying much too late at night. Julie, however, always got rid of her admirers as soon as I went to bed. She seemed to cling to me for protection—perhaps from her own weaknesses, though I was often embarrassed at having to listen to conversations that the young men would obviously have preferred alone with Julie. One of her swains, who used to bring his pair of spankers to take us for drives, suggested to her, in my hearing as usual, that she should give Charlie grounds for divorce by going to live with him and that they should then be married. I expected her to flare up with indignation, but she merely smiled like a sphinx.

I believed implicitly in her innocence until one day Percy turned up. 'Please let him stay the night,' one of the children asked me. 'He looks so funny in Mummie's nightgown!'

One after another my nurse-ladyhelps left because Julie snared their boy friends and my women patients dwindled because she captivated their husbands. On the other hand male patients besieged Dr House to admit them for undetectable complaints such as nervous breakdowns, sunstroke or heart trouble. He refused to do so, of course; and at one stage my patients were reduced to one man named Synot who had been kicked and mauled by a horse and was in plaster for weeks. He and his devoted brother who visited him daily both fell for Julie.

One night when we returned from a drive we stumbled over an apparently dead body in the dark hall. Seeing a flicker of light from the surgery, I decided there must have been an accident and that the doctor was in there fixing up the victims. When we found the surgery empty Julie became hysterical, and I was trembling from head to foot myself, when a thought struck me. I lit a candle and returned to 'the body' to find that it was, as I suspected, a dummy. On entering the ward I found my solitary patient in a seventh heaven of delight at the success of the joke that he and his brother had concocted for Julie's benefit.

Not long afterwards Julie asked me to mind the children for the day while she went to Perth to shop and see her husband. I telegraphed Charlie to meet her train but she eluded him, with the help of her gossamer veil, and met Percy instead. They then boarded a ship together and sailed for England.

Charlie came up and took the children and I never saw Julie again. Some time later, however, Percy returned to Australia a sadder and wiser man. He told us that soon after arriving in England Julie had left him for someone handsomer and wealthier. What she told her family goodness only knows, but it seems they received her back with open arms and thereafter blamed her colonial escapades on me.

The Katanning district hospital being by this time completed, there was too little business to justify my keeping on my nursing home so I sold up and went back to Applecross. I realised that I was hanging 'round the door of my third decade and that so far everything I had tried to build up had slipped from my fingers. Where had I gone wrong, I wondered, and what was I to do next?

Even Applecross was not developing as we had expected. A progressive speculator named Alexander Mathieson had bought up most of the land thereabouts and was responsible for many of the sites of the area being named after places in his native Scotland. A member of the State Senate he had a big voice in public affairs at that time and built himself a beautiful home at Coffee Point. The State, however, evidently failed to develop the locality as he had hoped and after succeeding to his father's title in 1920 he took himself off to greener fields.

Seven years after our home was completed, there were still only half a dozen houses along the high riverbank and it was clearly no place for young people to grow up. But far be it from Mother to admit it. 'A united family again,' she beamed, presiding at the round table that was laden as always with 'good wholesome food'.

Jack had just returned from Moora. He had found Bob down and out at a disreputable pub in Perth and had spent his last dollar bringing him home in a cab to avoid the shame of his being seen on the ferry.

Mother was happy to have Bob at her side again, away from temptation while he pulled himself together.

None of us was married yet and Mother treated us as though we were still in the nursery. After Bob went away to start again with the help of good friends in Albany, Jack, spoke up. 'Mother,' he said, 'the girls can't go on picking orchids along the riverbank, even if they do find a dozen different kinds as they often boast. If they're not going to marry they'll have to go to work. I've chewed this over and have a proposition to put to you. Sell this place and come up to Moora with me. I've seen a lawyer and fixed up an agreement to take over a property there.'

After much discussion, and on being assured that the house was comfortable and realising that dear Bob was as far from Moora as from Applecross, she agreed to help him when he had settled down. Estelle was then to take over our home, which was what Estelle wanted, and the other girls could do as they liked.

A local gossip columnist summed up our doings at that time in this way: 'Our Bob has disappeared again and Jack gone bush. Estelle, jilted, has jilted another, while Dollie clings to the arm of the law and Mollie refuses the hand of a well honoured citizen . . .'

I remember that piece of breezy impudence because of its smartness regarding Dollie who later married Max Law. The honoured citizen referred to was, I imagined, wooing Mother, for he was nearer her age and had grown-up children. I was most embarrassed when he proposed to me and quite appalled at the thought of taking on a man I did not love, and a ready made family to boot.

It was then that I felt again the Hand on my shoulder. As I was unable to write when anywhere near Mother and I loathed private nursing, I knew I must obtain a midwifery certificate. The catch was that I had no money and maternity schools were expensive and as far afield as Sydney and England in those days. But the Voice behind the Hand seemed to say: 'Leave it to me.'

Then the telephone rang and a friend said: 'Is that you, Mollie? Good. Well, you know everybody. Have you heard of anyone wanting to go to England who would take charge of children in return for her passage?'

'Yes,' I said. 'She's standing right here.'

10

The Hand on My Shoulder

The voyage started from Albany* on the south coast, where Bob had now found refuge. He was ashamed of me, for, having neither time nor money to get suitable clothes, I was travelling in nurse's uniform, with a suit and a couple of dinner dresses in my cabin trunk. This, with ten pounds in my pocket, pride in my bonnet and confidence in myself was all I needed—or so I thought as I stood on deck with my two small charges.

As we moved slowly out of the harbour into heavy seas, a stewardess came and took the children to their tea.

Our cabin was four-berthed with a porthole, and the children were there when I located it. Ella, the eldest, lay in the top berth playing the lady, Jill was asleep on the lower and Jackie screaming again, naked, amongst their day clothes, the whole place a wreck. Lifting the child, I asked Ella to start tidying up.

'That's your job,' she answered, putting her capable eleven-year-old hands complacently under her head.

When I asked her what she meant she pushed the bell for the stewardess and asked for a passenger list. This produced, she cast me a contemptuous look and read out: 'Mrs Key, five children and *nurse!*'

This meant I had no name, would have meals with the children and would be responsible for all five day and night, although two of the children shared their mother's cabin. In fact, though travelling first class, these businesslike people were saving twenty pounds on my fare by this arrangement.

* At that time steamers going to England from Australia via the Cape still called in at Albany, then calling only at Cape Town and the Canary Isles on the long voyage.

Though feeling like the devil about it, I was obliged to try to behave like an angel.

As the nights grew chilly with icy winds playing round the brilliantly illuminated little ship I had nowhere to retire to after the children were in bed but to the dining saloon. Oh, the dreariness of that deserted place! I couldn't even settle myself to write letters, as the long green baize-covered tables with chairs clamped alongside them swayed up and down like drunken horses, the doors slowly opening and closing but letting no human shape in or out.

All this had a queer effect on me and also gave me plenty of time to think and to commune with the unseen presence that I had come to think of as the Hand and the Voice. I suppose it was my conscience —'From a worldly point of view you will never be anyone or do anything of importance,' it seemed to say, 'but I will guide you where you are needed if you keep faith with me.'

These uplifting moments came to me quite frequently as the gathering clouds of fog heralded our approach to England. It was not, I should make clear, that I was religious in any orthodox way. In fact the very thought of 'religion' as such confused and baffled me. In Ireland, when snow made all the world a dazzling white, our nurse Loubie had taken us at Christmastime to see the crib of the Infant Jesus in the Roman Catholic church. His mother wore a crown; Saint Joseph had a crook and real lambs around him. There was a little donkey with a woven cross on his back, and hay in a box. Candles lit up the cobwebs so that they shone with shafts of gold and silver and when I looked up in delight, a priest laid hands on my hair and blessed me. I always felt sweet and soft and holy in that church. It was there, dressed in purple satin, all frills and fur-belows, with a little round hat of rosebuds and lace, that I acted as bridesmaid at the marriage of Loubie's soldier brother. Later in Scotland, sitting for hours every Sunday in a Presbyterian church in Edinburgh, I had felt hard and bored. I hated being forced to learn the Shorter Catechism that was so much longer than the Anglican one from which Bob and I had been taught before.

So there they were—three orthodox religions implanted in my very undeveloped mind. What wonder that I was confused? But the Hand was near when in my loneliness I leant on the rails at night. There was another comforting outcome of my loneliness and that was that the children came to love me. The babies clung to me and the little boys would give me nods of mischievous confidence, their hands touching me to show they would do as I said. Their parents hardly saw them on the voyage and as we neared our destination Mrs Key actually called me to her cabin to thank me for my assistance. When she said she had decided to recompense me for my services I hoped that this would be at least a part of the twenty pounds she had saved on my fare and that would have meant so much to me. Instead she pulled from her trunk a handsome woollen dress which she laid in my unwilling arms. 'This,' she said, 'should fit you quite nicely. I got it made when Jackie was on the way and have scarcely worn it.'

We were in the depth of winter when the ship's bells rang for the last time for us. We huddled into our warmest coats and scarves and ran down the gangway at Tilbury, where I looked forward to handing over the little 'milk buckets' to Grannie Key. This lady, however, soon showed that she had no intention of taking charge of them.

'My dear,' she told her daughter-in-law, 'I can't get a nursemaid. You'll have to go to a private hotel with this girl till we can secure one.'

Sorry as I was for Mrs Key, I was sorrier for myself. I just wasn't going to do it. I had been waiting in a sort of strangled agony of impatience for the moment when I could be myself again, free to go to my own relations and set about the work I had come so far to embark on. My heart sang at the mere thought of seeing the familiar faces of the nurses I had loved so well eight years before.

When I woke next morning in the double bed with Jack and Jill, Mrs Key came in, leading the two boys who looked rather shabby in outgrown coats, blue jerseys and knickerbockers. 'After breakfast,' she announced, 'we will get a cab to Swan & Edgars to rig out the children in some new clothes.'

I smiled, the name of that store reminding me of the two black swans that came every year to our little bay at Applecross and which Daddy had dubbed 'Swan and Edgar'.

When the five children and their mama were seated on chairs in the boots and shoes department with attendants kneeling before them and brandishing shoe-horns, the fifth sparrow, feeling that she had done all that was necessary, spread her wings and flew.

I boarded a twopenny bus and felt as much at home as when I had done so eight years before. Eros a-top his fountain was still surrounded by flower-women, the roads were still floored with jarrah blocks from our south-western forests, the same old Marble Arch, Regent Street, Oxford Circus, and at last—Bayswater.

And then I was being hugged by my little Aunt Minnie, hub of the wheel of the Skinner family and still holding the money bags. She had promised Father that I should never want. She welcomed me warmly to the flat where she now lived with Alice the faithful maid and a Pekinese dog.

'We must arrange for you to get this training at Queen Charlotte's Hospital,' she said, when I explained my purpose.

'It's hardly likely there would be a vacancy,' I replied, 'and besides I've only got ten pounds.'

Aunt Minnie then took me to William Whiteley's great store and rigged me out before taking me to see my eldest cousin, Colonel (later General) Bruce Skinner, R.A.M.C., who was at the time in charge of Millbank Military Hospital, on the Embankment.

The visit led to my receiving a letter from another more distant relation named Miss Becher, head of Queen Alexandra's Nursing Service, who asked me to call on her at the War Office.

She was horrified when I informed her that I wanted to be a *midwife*, but my explanations rather amused her.

'I can get you into a Military Families Hospital in two months' time,' she told me, after consulting a file. 'The training is free but the outfit is expensive and you will need ample pocket money to keep up appearances during your year with them.'

When I explained that I had only ten pounds in the world, she merely smiled. Then she wrote down my name and said she would notify me when the vacancy occurred.

On the way out I met an old friend, Colonel MacPherson, who bore me off to lunch at the Trocadero.

'You know, Mollie, you're not a day older than when we first met you. You're too unsophisticated to be let run loose in London. Come down and stay with us at Chorley whenever you feel like it. There'll always be a bed for you.'

He looked dubious when I told him I was to start training at a Families Hospital. 'If you stick to your own ideas you may be all right,' he said. 'Try not to annoy Miss Becher, though how you can avoid it I'm hanged if I know.'

That I might annoy Miss Becher did not trouble me in the least, but the idea of waiting to do so for two months did. It would be impossible to stay all that time in what seemed to me the prison of my dear little aunt's flat. Aunt Minnie realised it too and wrote to her brothers who immediately invited me to stay in succession at their homes.

I went first to my pious Uncle Evelyn ('The Black Heathen') for Easter, and while there received a postcard which I have always treasured. The message reads: 'Deb and I sail "Artonia" in March 15th inst. Deb will go with three children to Tilbury. I shall probably cross from Marseilles. Deb very well. Address Agent-General. 1/3/'09. J.W.H.' J.W.H. was John Winthrop Hackett, and his wife my beloved friend Deborah.

On the evening of their arrival I dined with them at some grand hotel where after consulting the magnificent bill of fare my host chose a kippered herring. 'I've been longing for a real Irish kipper ever since I went to Australia,' he said. And there he sat, to the embarrassment of his wife and the maître d'hôtel, in his starched shirt and dinner jacket, declining the chef's culinary triumphs for this homely fare.

One day during my time of waiting to enter the Families Hospital I noticed an advertisement in a paper I took named *The Hospital*:

> £10 bonus offered to trained nurse for C.M.B. on District principles. Apply 63 Myddleton Square, S.E.

I applied for this position then and there and later showed it to Aunt Minnie. She shook her head. 'Have nothing to do with it—probably white slave traffic,' she said.

'*The Hospital* is a most respectable journal,' I cried, 'I'm sure it's genuine.'

'It's not the *Church Times*, dear,' she said.

In reply I received a courteous letter signed Sybil Avis Dauney, pointing out that the advertisement was obsolete, the journal having been to Australia and back. Aunt Minnie was relieved, but handed the advertisement to her clergyman to investigate.

I was not unduly amazed, however, when soon afterwards I received another letter from Miss Dauney to say that the pupil who had been booked for the vacancy had fallen out, and as the four months' training requisite for the C.M.B. had started, the committee, to save a deadlock, offered it to me.

So there I was on the doorstep of Myddleton Square behind the Angel Islington, looking at the trees which were springing to leaf in the Square garden.

Through the intuition given me by semi-blindness and an unusual upbringing, I sensed that I had come here to learn charity, although I did not know till then that I lacked it. When my eyes fell on Miss Dauney I knew that she would teach it me. She was slight, slim and still, her face oval with patrician features and with tendrils of dark hair round the forehead. Her green-flecked eyes held almost saintly tranquillity until they lit with flashes of human understanding. She was like the Virgin on the medal she had designed for the Association and engraved with the words: 'The love of Christ constraineth us.'

I learnt later that, not unlike Florence Nightingale, she had been brought up by worldly folk who resented her calling. She had trained at St. Bartholomew's Hospital, gone to the war in South Africa, and now devoting her life to mothers and babies found her strength and consolation in the Anglo-Catholic religion. She was interested in culture in all forms and had a keen sense of humour, handling the riff-raff of sinful women who came to book in as if they were angels, and was sweet to the disapproving Protestant nurses.

There were three midwives, two lecturing doctors and a visiting student-sister, Miss Ostle, to coach for the difficult C.M.B. examination. More than 160 maternity cases had to be booked for every four months, as each pupil had to 'conduct' twenty cases herself before taking the exam and quite a few babies were born before the pupil's arrival (B.B.A.).

At first I registered to nothing but dashing off at nights with the chief midwife, Sister Huxtable; coming down to breakfast after being out all night; trudging off with another pupil to nurse every morning and evening in all weathers; sterilising, repacking and renewing contents of bags daily; attending lectures and learning off reels of terms and tabulations (mostly in Latin), and maintaining self-discipline amongst squalor and fear, however the nerves were stretched.

In the rush and tear of training I remember distinctly only my first two conductions—not in the slums proper but on their fringes. The first delighted me. It was in the Italian quarter down Little Saffron Hill, a cobbled street with small three-storied houses packed side by side below Holborn Viaduct. To go there was to take an

The author, about the time of her meeting with D. H. Lawrence in 1922

The author, seventy years of age, at the time of writing *The Fifth Sparrow*

Birthplace of Mollie Skinner—the Officers Quarters, St. George's Terrace, Perth

Sir John and Lady Winthrop Hackett c. 1900 when they first met the author

Colonel and Mrs James Skinner and five of their seven children, Ireland 1882. Mollie is on the left leaning against the tree

Hotel Garcia · Guadalajara · Jal · Mexico
15th Novem · 1923

Dear Miss Skinner
            I finished the novel
yesterday. I call it _The Boy in the Bush_. I
think quite a lot of it. Today I am sending
the MS. to my agent, Curtis Brown
                        6 Henrietta St
                            Covent Garden
                                London W.C. 2.
His cable address is Browncurt. London.
Curtis Brown will have the MS typed, & the moment
I get to London — I hope to be there by Christmas — I
will go through it & have a copy sent to you.
            Seltzer wants to do the book in
New York in April. so that would mean Martin Secker
bringing it out at the same time in London. Seltzer
suggests my name & yours as joint authors.
            I shall wait to hear from
you.
            Yours sincerely
                D H Lawrence

D. H. Lawrence's letter of 15 November 1923 to Mollie Skinner

By
D.H.
Lawrence
and
M.L.
Skinner

The
Boy
In
The
Bush

Brett

Jacket of the American edition of *The Boy in the Bush*

South-west district hospital of which the author was matron in 1923

Group Settlement in the south-west in 1923—a scheme 'too hastily and optimistically devised'

40 &5

~~when you are introduced, but never after when you meet).~~

"Excuse me a minute, Ted, I - "

"Right you are, Jim." [Ted Horton] ~~He~~ stood still and ~~they~~ passed on.

~~I saw~~ Jim waved friends off like flies (it was a Saturday morning and men were not working) and ~~I~~ [Evelyn] felt he was straining like a ship at anchor set with sails to be off in the breeze. But for a few moments more ~~she~~ would be his anchor ...

There now, the account was fixed. [Evelyn] ~~I~~ walked back alone to the hospital. Jim walked up towards the iron building that served as hotel, and men surrounded him. He had said goodbye to her nicely, with his slow, polite smile. But somehow [she] ~~I~~ was not satisfied. He certainly treated her as a mate, not as a butting-in woman, still - still not as a woman at all. Curious, none of these men - except Reeve's and perhaps Sandyman, the only ones [she] ~~I~~ disliked - looked on her as a woman. [Yet she was attractive - had allure.] Oh, well, just as well perhaps ...

Every one loved Jim - all his mates. Two or three were always hanging round the place waiting for him. They ~~would~~ all ask him to drink, and then suggest that he camps with them, individually. Not altogether disinterested perhaps. They got a good lot out of him, and besides, he was a "sport"; he had that attraction for men that comes from a courageous, emotional nature; he was silently sympathetic, and always did and said the right thing at the right moment. And then he had his pension of twenty-five ~~Rose took to spending her time before the surgery~~ shillings a week, the Government's compensation for his mortal hurt - and that was extraordinarily useful as a lever to get stores with. "There you are, Mr. McFee", they would say to the storekeeper, "I'm camping up with Jim, and if we can't scrape up a bit o' dust to settle with you later, there's always Jim's pension."

A page from Mollie Skinner's unpublished novel *Eve in the Land of Nod*

Sunday 21 -10 -39
Darlington

My dear Mary,

I can't help writing to you about the letter in yesterday's "West" "help & letter" re your story. What I want to convey is a peculiar sort of congratulation, that you have touched the heart of your readers. If you have that gift — as you have that gift nothing must stop you! — not marriage, or Palaces, or war, or anything. And it won't for you have marriage and Palaces and war and everything — all in a year — and one feels that it has 'grown' the "it". One can see that in your eye, and in your manner, and your surprised innocent smile. This is, then congratulations.

yours affectionately

Mollie Skinner.

A letter to Mary Durack from Mollie Skinner, 21 October 1939 excursion into a toy Italy. Sister Huxtable told me to mind my step when nursing these passionate people and to observe their customs as far as possible. Papa was the menace and must be kept out of the room, but his or her Mama must be permitted to remain and would usually help.

My next conduction was somewhere at the back of the Angel in Islington in a continuous row of houses fenced by iron railings with locked gates. It was a gloomy limbo of a place, absolutely deserted and lit only by a watery moon above the sooty chimney stacks. On and on we trailed, Father slipping and sliding through the shadows just ahead of us, until, gesturing for us to wait, he stooped, lifted the lid of a coal chute and disappeared into it.

Even Nurse Fields, my dour and experienced companion, was nonplussed. She went to the nearest gate and finding it locked pulled a bell, which came away in her hand. Presently Father came up the steps from the basement and attacked the gate with a jemmy. 'I'll mend the bell termorrer,' he said as we passed inside.

A woman called Mamie met us at the back door and showed us up a dark stairway and into a room that took one back half a century. It must have been furnished by the prosperous draper who formerly ran the shop underneath in High Street, for it had an Axminster carpet, early Victorian hangings, heavy mantel and feather bed. We discovered later that the shops were now entirely disconnected from the houses above which had degenerated into a rabbit warren of the the underworld.

Fields took a strong dislike to the feather mattress and told me to remove it and make the bed up on the horsehair under it, an order that brought Cockney curses from the handsome young patient whom we found striding the floor.

Getting the twenty conductions required for the C.M.B. examination in less than four months meant continuous and exhausting work. We found it stimulating enough but were all more or less dazed and in a state of high tension when we faced the exams at last—two written papers (midwifery and maternity nursing) and a viva.

Discussing our papers afterwards it appeared, as my companions agreed, that I had failed. Then came the viva when, bluffing like a puffed up frilled lizard, I faced the three eminent physicians.

'What would you do if you found the child in transverse position?' I was asked.

I prepared to scuttle, my frill folding around my neck. 'Send for a doctor,' I stuttered, 'and if he didn't come pray for a spontaneous rectification.'

The doctor in the middle adjusted his eyeglass and looked at me. 'Pray?' he ejaculated. 'Where do you come from?'

'Australia.'

He tapped the paper in front of him and smiled. 'Oh indeed! So the Salvation Army has reached the Antipodes. And what would you do if you found the patient haemorrhaging before the fifth month?'

My mind flashed to some of Julie's stories of the goldfields—cases of abortion that had been tragic for both mother and 'nurse'.

'I'd walk out of the house,' I said.

The examiners glanced at each other and smiled.

So dejectedly I faced Miss Dauney and told her I had failed and hadn't a penny in my pocket. I told her that a Perth friend Mr A. O. Neville, then in the Agent General's office in the Strand, had promised to give me first option to take charge of the next group of emigrant women going to Western Australia and that while waiting for this I would return to my relatives. I am sure she understood how I hated being dependent, even for a short time, on my father's family.

A day or two later came a telegram from Miss Dauney:

YOU TOPPED EXAMINATION LIST CALL IMMEDIATELY DISCUSS PROPOSITION

As Sister Huxtable had taken over a new branch of the Association at Camden Town, I was offered the vacancy at Myddleton Square to gain experience at £30 a year and 'all found'.

I said I would take it immediately but Miss Dauney said I must first have a holiday.

'Holiday!' I exclaimed, my whirl of exultation giving place to sudden anger at the thought of trying to relax with my uncles' wives and children who despised me and the work I had espoused.

Miss Dauney's look silenced and shamed me. 'I'll put your name down to take up duty on the last day of August. You must take that holiday, my dear.'

Autumn was passing into winter when my term as midwife began. The trees in the Square turned black and bare like Australian trees in the wake of a bushfire. Icy winds tossed our cloaks aside and battered through our cotton dresses, frosts bit at our cheeks and hands, but we were all, I think, profoundly happy that year at Myddleton Square. Under the direction of Miss Dauney—or Sybil, as I now called her—our training ran smoothly.

In January I was sent off as second midwife to the Camden Town branch, where the work was easier and in better homes, but far less interesting. The new 'free medicine' and medical laws had now come into practice and we worked mostly under doctors who were engaged to preside, at a small fee.

Here I had two upsetting experiences, the first in a case of delayed labour, when the doctor, hurrying off to a well-to-do patient, left myself and a trainee nurse in charge.

Hour after hour passed without further progress, the mother weakening. An examination revealed that the baby's arm, instead of being folded on the chest, had fallen across the head, but my urgent note to the doctor brought forth only the cryptic reply: 'Draw it down. Can't come.'

I drew it down and broke that little arm. I shall never forget the crack or the horror I felt at seeing it, though the child was perfect in every other way.

The other case was when we called on a patient, who had given birth two days before, to find the baby dead under the mother's breast. It was I who had to face the coroner, and that gave me the horrors. The doctor, mother and Association were cleared of all blame.

Human love is inspiring in whatever form it be, and the Devil himself knows it and lays hands on it to twist it out of the Divine Pattern, if he can. But the Devil did not have a chance against Sybil Avis Dauney when she loved and nurtured this fifth sparrow that had fallen into her care. Her influence made me consider myself an Anglo-Catholic. When under her benign influence knowing the holy joy of a Oneness with Father, Son and Holy Spirit, I thought I could carry on in the same way when I returned to Australia.

You may wonder how I could consider going back when I had found my medium, with happy companionship and fullness of life. Now into my thirties, I had no desire for marriage or children, for money or worldly pleasures. I enjoyed nothing more than being with Sybil, doing the work she was doing. I loved her as I had never loved a woman before, and I was never to love anyone again in quite the same way. But I could not escape the fact that the core of my being was in Western Australia. I felt drawn to it as an Aboriginal is drawn to his spirit country—or was it that the Hand on my shoulder was pushing me back where I belonged?

When a letter came from the Agent General's office inviting me to take charge of one hundred and four emigrant girls on their way to Fremantle I accepted the offer, noting as I did so that I had landed in England exactly a year before.

11

Emigrants

How could one person have been expected to look after one hundred and four happy, undisciplined girls among three hundred third class passengers, with another hundred emigrant lads stowed amidships?

My girls had beds slung in four adjacent compartments in the hold, my cabin, till I made a row about it, the only means of air for all. It was suffocating with the door shut and was moreover the home of the ship's cats.

My complaint annoyed the purser, but in the end I was given a stewardess's cabin above. The stewardesses, with whom I dined in the second class saloon after the passengers, resented me and my brood. I was placed below the salt—which more often than not they forgot to pass to me.

In theory the voyage was organised to be a happy one—and in practice it proved so with the help of a huge workbox. The girls had meals after the other third class passengers and were forbidden to mix with the crowd on deck. But the tricks they were up to! After one petty officer was caught holding out his arms for a girl to jump into down the gangway, the officers and even the stewards were under orders not to speak to the girls on pain of dismissal, or loss of promotion.

A girl named Gertie, a fine type of yeoman's daughter and full of laughter, soon became a great help to me. I needed it, for it was impossible to get these girls together on the crowded decks. While I was settling arguments concerning the possession of quoits between some of my girls and third class passengers, Gertie would be separating fighting factory girls.

At the beginning of the voyage I asked them what they had been and they told me factory hands, domestics, tailoresses, cotton spinners, pottery workers. There was no variety, however, about what they intended doing in Australia. One and all answered the query with a merry laugh, pointing to a clause in the printed paper which read something like this: 'There are hundreds of miners, tradesmen, artisans etc. earning good wages in Western Australia who are seeking wives of sound health and cheerful disposition.'

The captain would not allow my girls to land at any port, though the sea was anathema to them. As we passed the Suez Canal and wilted in the Red Sea, the whole mob sat down and wept. I grew anxious, for temperatures rose, pulses quickened and weakened, and the sick bay had to be opened for treatment. Gertie was invaluable and full of common sense. 'Tell Cap to let 'em off at the next port, Sister, and they'll get well, pronto.'

The captain was far too high and mighty to be approached by me, while the doctor, whom I begged to intercede, was on board only for that voyage and had little influence.

As we approached Colombo a girl called Amy developed alarming symptoms and broke out in a pox. The doctor isolated her with me and reported to the captain. Smallpox on the maiden voyage of the *Osterley*? Unlikely, since everyone else was in excellent health, all the emigrants had been vaccinated and none of them had been ashore. The Colombo health authorities, however, decided that Amy must be rushed to quarantine, accompanied by myself. At this the captain put his foot down. He would not, for all the tea in China, take those hundred and four girls on without their matron in charge. Orders came from the bridge that I was to return after the patient was placed in quarantine.

None of the other girls were visible when Amy and I left the ship but as the ambulance, after a long delay on the wharf, drove through the streets, there they all were, like a swarm of bees in search of a new hive.

Amy, left in a charming open-air room with a Singhalese nurse to fan her, thought she was in heaven, except for the fact that a girl named Hester had the key of her box. I thought I was in the other place when I sallied forth again into the city and eight girls ringed my rickshaw, shouting.

Recognising one as Hester, I yelled to her to give me the key of Amy's box, but she didn't hear me and the next moment had flung herself into the arms of a British Tommy on sentry duty. Another flung her arms around the neck of my rickshaw man who was so scared he ran away. The other six, still holding hands, played stringy-meat down the road. I fled into the bazaar to have a cool drink and found the whole place alive with rollicking emigrant girls and boys. Turning tail, I ran into Gertie.

'It's no good trying to do anything,' she said in her matter of fact way. 'Let's go back to the ship and get officials on the job. They all went mad and broke for shore on a tender as soon as you left.'

We took a gharry back to the wharf, passing our girls, some arm in arm with soldiers and sailors, some grouped round stalls drinking pernicious native drinks and eating over-ripe fruit bought from native vendors, others drawing rickshaws with the rickshaw boys as passengers.

Down in the hold I found a raging stewardess surrounded by Singhalese boys demanding payment for the girls' washing which they had delivered back spick and span to the ship.

Leaving the poor woman to cope, I went to the purser's office, where I was handed government instructions from Western Australia including a parliamentary letter of thanks and a cheque for myself for £2/2/6d.

'Please, Mr Purser,' I implored, 'ring the police station to have those girls brought back to the wharf.'

He regarded me with contempt. 'That's not the ship's business. You are solely responsible for them on land and the captain is furious. We sail in half an hour regardless of whether we carry them or not.'

Struck to the heart, I leant over the rail and watched the first, second, and last tender bringing back passengers—but not one emigrant girl.

Then, miraculously, there were at least some of the girls paying for their washing, the stewardess now grinning at their fun. Then Gertie came down the gangway, shepherding some twenty more.

'How on earth did you get aboard?' I asked.

'Hired a couple of boats. The harbour's dotted with them.'

After this outburst the girls were subdued and obedient. They asked for needlework and sat at it diligently. They did not fight among themselves, argue with the third class women, sit on their husbands' knees, or share deck chairs with the boys.

Towards the end of the voyage one of the older girls came to me with a young man and asked me to request the captain to marry them. I told the man he must make the request himself. He did so and then the captain sent for me. He told me such a marriage was impossible. Then he sent the purser out of the office, took me by the shoulders and shook me, laughing till the tears ran down his cheeks. 'This voyage has been an ordeal for me from first to last, Sister. It's nearly over now without mutiny and without smallpox. Word has come through that the girl we left in Colombo is all right. I can't say any more.' He blew his nose and stalked away.

On the wharf at Fremantle I heaved a sigh of relief but my charges were plunged into the depths of gloom. 'We want to go 'ome. 'What sort of place is this you've brought us to?' 'Where are our 'usbands?' And then Gertie called out, 'All we want is letters from home to show they've not forgotten us.' A chorus went up: 'Where's our letters? Ain't the mail in yet?'

To subdue them I called out, 'Don't be silly, this ship carried the mails.'

There was a yell of laughter. 'And it brought the females too.' Then they all began to sing.

12

On Dangerous Ground

Jack drove his spanking pair of horses to Moora to meet me. As we drove back to Berkshire Valley he pointed out how one property after another had failed for want of rain. Harvests had withered, cattle had died, the weakened sheep and lambs fallen a prey to dingoes. When he took over the property the drought had been in its fifth year but up to that time his place had not suffered terribly. Now, two years later, they had still had no rain and the whole country was parched. Jack, always full of hope, was battling on like a Trojan with the help of a mate named Wentworth Single.

'I came here in my socks,' he said, as we drove along, 'and at the end of the year I'll walk out in them if the rains hold off this season. Still, I'll hand in my contract with exactly the same number of sheep and cattle I took over, as I had enough hay to handfeed them and we dug a well in the riverbank—hit a fresh spring with the help of a divining rod.'

Mother and Mittie were at the house. It was a comfortable place and they were enjoying themselves despite the hard times. It was good to be back with them and surrounded by the bush I loved, but hard to close my eyes to the tragedy of it all. Most of the neighbouring farmers were bankrupt and one by one leaving their properties.

Not long after my arrival a family named Stokes invited us to a farewell party. Old Joe Stokes had started out as a shepherd, married and had sons, taken up a property, shepherded his own sheep and made a fortune. Foolishly he had gambled on the seasons and done nothing to conserve water so that now just as his sons had grown up he had no sheep left and was preparing to pack up and walk out.

But there was nothing miserable about that farewell gathering. We all played cricket and everyone laughed themselves sick when I ran after the ball in my fashionable hobble-skirt. Then we sat down to a sumptuous repast, eating the last of the ham, the last fowls, the last leg of mutton, the last bread, scones and cakes Mum Stokes would ever bake on that farm and drained the last keg of wine. Afterwards Joe took up his fiddle and we jigged and sang songs until it was too late to go home. The men camped on the floor and the women arranged themselves crossways like logs on the old double bed.

Jack still went on breaking in horses that were sent him for that purpose from agents who bought them cheap from bankrupt farmers. I saw him come over the head of one of these buckjumpers, the saddle between his knees and he still on his feet.

We went to church together in the Road Board hall in Moora, Jack in a snow-white suit and a straw hat perched on his close-cropped head. While singing, 'Can a mother's tender care cease towards the child she bear?' he stooped to whisper in my ear, 'Never mind about the *he* bear!' (The old conflict between Jack and Mother was silent now, but always there.)

Glimpses of Jack at that time haunt my memory—his masterly control of the rearing horses when the shaft of the buggy broke; replacing the shaft with a felled sapling and harnessing up again; taking us down to the lower paddock where he and his mate were digging another well, going down the hole and coming up grinning with a mug of water that was as salt as the sea.

'That's our last hope, Mother,' he said. 'You and the girls will have to go back to Applecross, and we'll go off to Bullfinch prospecting.'

They did and when the war came they joined the forces and went away with empty pockets but as always the joy of living in their hearts.

When I got back to Perth I found that a fine old doctor friend had died, instructing his brother to offer me his nursing home at a minimal rent of two pounds per week. I was delighted, though as the place was not in the west end the fashionable doctors never patronised it. It consisted of ten furnished wards, a well fitted operating room complete with modern steriliser and rooms for the staff. But . . .

I had no money, and the previous matron had written to a lawyer saying that the beds and furniture belonged to her. The lawyer arranged a sale of these effects and hoping to purchase them myself

I went round with the hat to my rich relations. They looked down their noses and sent me off with a flea in my ear, at which Mother, in her pride and dignity, was annoyed—not with them, but with me. The sparrow was down and well pecked, but soon rose and found a partner (whom I will call Winnie), an elderly widow who agreed to put in cash against my goodwill.

My partner got the furniture for seventy pounds, a sum I remember well because Winnie immediately began to hold it over me like a whip. Soon after we took over and I was washing the stairs she sneered that the linen cupboard was empty and the blankets thin. What was I going to do about it? I kicked the bucket downstairs and said I would provide seventy pounds worth of sheets and blankets and to hell with her, then went straight off to Charles Moore and Co., where Mother had an account, and put my case before the manager. Would he let me have seventy pounds worth of sheets and blankets on a bond of faith? He did.

After this Winnie behaved only as badly as she dared, as she could see money in the partnership. At the end of the year all debts were paid and we were clearing seventy pounds a week profit.

There were bright passages connected with this period. Many good doctors conducted their maternity cases and operations there with excellent results. It was there I had my first experience in the use of the new 'twilight sleep' to relieve the suffering of childbirth, there that my sister Nazeli had her first baby and Dollie a minor operation. But there was a darker side that led me to suspect and finally to know that my little hospital was being used by certain unscrupulous doctors for ends to which I could not be a part.

One doctor arranged for his patients to pay him a fee for their treatment from which, in cases of surgery, he paid us a round sum for three weeks in advance—adding as he did so 'for better or worse'. A publican's wife on whom he performed a major operation succumbed three days later, due, I believed, to his neglect of symptoms we had pointed out to him. When I protested he merely shrugged. 'What have *you* got to complain about?' he asked. 'Three days' nursing and you've been paid for three weeks.'

The end of my association with this doctor was after he had admitted an old man named Sims, who had been dying slowly and contentedly of cancer in his own home, on the assurance that an operation would give him a new lease of life. When I asked the doctor whether he believed he could do anything to help him, he breathed in my ear: 'Fifty pounds in my pocket and thirty in yours when I open the golden gates for him tomorrow.' I told Mrs Sims to save her money and take her old man home and let him die in peace and very pleased she was to do so.

I soon came to distinguish the doctors of integrity from those better described as 'quacks'. One of the latter kind sent in a peroxide blonde of uncertain years, named Mrs Smith. The woman was prepared, according to instructions, for an abdominal operation after which her devoted husband sat by, holding her hand until the doctor arrived with a second physician. They sent the man out of the room and me also. I could scarcely believe it when I returned later to find they had produced a baby which I at once began trying to resuscitate. To my horror I was forcibly ejected from the room.

That night a strange man arrived at the door, saying that he was Mr Smith and had called to see his wife who had been operated on that morning. He had just returned from England after a year's absence.

I told him she was all right but that her doctor had forbidden any visitors at all for some days and I could not let him in without permission. He shook my hand, greatly relieved, leaving me the limp instrument of evil doings.

That quack had a young qualified assistant named, let us say, Jim who had evidently got himself into deep water and was perhaps the victim of blackmail. One morning he brought in a man in a comatose condition for whom he demanded a private room and prescribed the treatment appropriate for one at death's door. Jim, pale and trembling, instructed me that I special him myself and let no one else near him, explaining that he was a poor down-and-out, the victim of some accident who had been brought to his surgery. As I sat with the poor fellow during his last hours he babbled about having taken on night work at the lime kilns at half pay and had been set upon as a 'scab'. Peppered with shot, he knew no more than having the shot removed from his groin in a surgery. He died that night, flotsam on the sea of life, whose story will never now be known.

I was sorry for Jim as although apparently a weak character, he was not unfeeling and often worked with doctors of good repute. With one of these he performed an operation on a pretty young seamstress with a growth. As she went on the table she cried out that she wouldn't have it done and to leave her be, but Jim persuaded her it was for her good. He was wrong, and he nearly went frantic when it was found that she was dying. He brought her champagne and sat by her day and night until the end and paid all hospital and funeral expenses. I think he must have been in love with her, as he went away soon afterwards, quite broken, to another state.

I became expert at what my family called 'fibrication'. On one occasion a doctor called to say he was sending in a case of pneumonia. He told us that all enquiries concerning her were to be answered with the assurance that she was 'progressing favourably' and that she was to receive no visitors for ten days. He brought the girl in, confined her and told me that a woman would call for the baby in the evening. The child was adopted and I could only congratulate that doctor for his quiet diplomacy, but the young patient was well known and popular and my tongue grew pimples answering the calls of enquiry.

To take my mind off such tragedies I set to work and wrote a midwifery text book for nurses, which was later published by Tindall and Cox and brought me in royalties for many years.

Sybil Dauney wrote me letters full of inspiration and sent me prayers which, although when removed from her influence I had not continued to practise her Anglo-Catholic faith, were my greatest comfort.

One night while dozing by an unconscious patient I had a dream —or perhaps a vision—of Sybil, beautifully dressed as if for some social function. She held out her hands to me and said: 'My dear, I have to leave you now.' 'But it's I who have left you,' I said and started awake to tend my patient.

Next night, sitting within hearing of all calls, dozing but alert to the slightest sound, I felt myself floating over the ocean, drawn by a silver cord and knowing that Sybil held the other end. It snapped and I rose with such a bewildering sense of loss that I wrote in my notebook the hour and the date. It corresponded exactly with the hour of her death of which I heard from her sister by the following mail. At the same time I received a letter from Sybil herself. It was unsigned as though she had intended adding to it when she was called away. It ended with a quotation from Francis Thompson's 'The Hound of Heaven':

> Is my gloom, after all,
> Shade of His hand, outstretched caressingly?

Her death had a curious effect on me. It was the end of my interest in the nursing home. Without the slightest compunction I left thirty pounds a week for thirty pounds a year to work in the London slums again, but jingling for the first time in my life a handsome sum of money in my pocket.

13

Breaking Point

This time the journey to England was smooth sailing. I felt so clever, for I had written a text-book that was to be published, and turned my back on money and prosperity. I might not be good-looking or young any more but I was going to make a saint of myself in the slums of London which everyone would say was noble even if ill-advised. My ego was rampant and full of cheer.

Dr Kelsall and his wife, my Aunt Blanche, were taking their daughter Peggy to finish her education at Home. Travelling with them were Tommie Riley, the Archbishop's son (himself to become a bishop) and the two Merry girls, Gracie and Vi. (The latter became the mother of Shirley Strickland of Olympic running fame.) Together with one or two other young men we were called 'the vice-regal party'. On such jolly journeys the world's concerns are thrown overboard as we found a crazy old salt throwing the cups and saucers, spoons and books left on deck. Once I caught him about to heave overboard the precious volume of Oxford Book of English Verse, which Tommie and I had been gloating over.

'Hey!' I remonstrated just in time to save it. 'So that's where our things go when left on deck?'

'It's for them poor corpses, miss,' he said, ''eavin' round in Davey Jones's locker with nothing to amuse themsels with.'

Not that I had much use for poetry when we reached London. In fact I soon wondered why on earth I had returned. Sybil Dauney was dead and I had not realised how much my happiness in the old job at Myddleton Square had depended on her. The cold, the wet, the fog and icy winds ate into body and mind and instead of finding love in the work again, I lost it.

I fell into step with Miss Muriel and another capable sister who had taken Sybil's place at Myddleton Square. Two new midwives took round the pupils who were of the new order of Queen's District Nurses (a great organisation started by Queen Mary), applicants of the Colonial Hospitals or for Lady Minto's Private Nursing Service in India.

Although I had been trained in London and held the C.M.B. certificate, I was looked on as an Australian. The British Nurses Registration Board did not recognise Australian nurses at that time, and vice versa. By sheer good luck, however, when back in Australia the year before I had managed to register with the A.T.N.A. without retraining, by passing the vivas. I was a first-rate midwife and so was tolerated.

Then my arm was smitten with neuritis and pain and fear gat hold upon me. Supposing I lost my job, what would I do? My cash was spent. It was hopeless to think of taking up writing in London—for me at any rate (Katharine Susannah Prichard was earning her living this way at the time, but I did not know her then).

There had been no spring in my step, no love in my heart, when early one morning, feeling physically ill and the pain of neuritis at its height, I accompanied a pupil to a conduction in a slum area. The mother, no longer young, already burdened with too many children and desperately poor, had a long hard labour and I found myself thinking it would be a good thing if the child was born dead. It was not, as it happened, and as I placed the little scrap in its mother's arms she smiled at me with such love and gratitude that the tears rushed to my eyes. I sent my pupil home and stayed on a while.

On the hall table back at Myddleton Square was a letter from my publishers, enclosing a cheque with a letter from an eminent doctor expressing admiration of my midwifery book and asking whether they would publish one by himself on the same lines but for general use. This gave me confidence enough to visit an old nursing friend named Miss Thomas-Moore—or Tommie as we called her—who was now in charge of a grand nursing home in Berkeley Square.

She laughed at my book and asked me seriously to give up slumming and join her in the new venture, a modern hospital then being built for her near Harley Street. She said the doctors we had known when working together had often asked for me, and she seemed almost impatient with me when I shook my head. She did not realise that my spirit was then almost broken and my body too.

On the way back to Myddleton Square I managed to stagger from the bus and cling to a lamp post where I wished I could die. Instead I vomited. When sitting in a semi-dazed state at the bus stop I felt a hand on my shoulder—in this case a human one belonging to Charlie Osborne, a young friend from Western Australia. He had come over 'to see the sights' and here he was seeing one he had not bargained on.

He took me in a cab to my little Aunt Minnie who for once put her dainty foot firmly down. In no time she had me in bed under the care of a nurse and a doctor who backed her up in everything she said. My appointment at Myddleton Square was cancelled, and I found myself on a liner for India with a cousin, Monica Gough, who planned to take me on for a trip to Kashmir. The Hand was on my shoulder again and joy in my heart.

14

Indian Interlude

On landing in Calcutta, completely recovered but my pockets empty, I called on Mrs Davis, the Superintendent of Lady Minto's Nursing Service that had been formed for soldiers and their families by the wife of Lord Minto who was then Viceroy of India. I was told that a sister was wanted urgently at Rawalpindi near the frontier, which assignment I accepted then and there.

From this centre I nursed cases at Peshawar at the end of the Indian Railway; at Bunnu, over the Indus; the Malakand Fort across the border; Lahore and other exciting places of which I later wrote in my novel *Tucker Sees India* which was published by Secker and Warburg in 1937.

Thus in a few months I saw India as few have seen it—not the famine stricken or the wealthy India, but the beautiful India below great mountains loved by countless men and women from biblical days. Here my heart expanded. I began to love at last with true charity, and was filled with happiness. It was easy to be happy, for a Minto Sister was treated by everyone with honour and respect. Besides, in almost every cantonment I found a cousin attached to the regiment. One was a Q.A.M.N.S. Sister, Evelyn Skinner, who being of my own build and colouring and never wearing her beautiful clothes more than once or twice in the same society, generously passed them on to me. As I was moving about from place to place I could appear everywhere as though in possession of a splendid Parisian wardrobe.

In Kashmir I stayed with my cousin Monica in a houseboat on the Shalamar Lake. Lotus lilies, temple bells, snow-covered mountains —oh, what on earth so lovely!

From here I was sent to Old Delhi to nurse at the only hospital staffed by Minto Sisters—the Hindu Rao which had been set apart for officials on the hill near Vice-regal Lodge. There were only three

Sisters in charge, the nursing being done by orderlies and trained Indian servants, so it was a post to which all the Minto Sisters ardently aspired. In fact vibrations reached me that by being sent there I had gained sixty lynx-eyed enemies. 'It isn't fair, she's an Australian, a recent joinee, a flat-footed jane without dignity or prestige in the Service. Let's be rid of her . . .'

However, it was not so easy as I soon made friends with Miss Dalrymple who was in charge and who enjoyed the social life in Delhi to the full. She rode, was a crack shot at the rifle range, a guest at smart dinners and picnics, persona grata at the Club and a humorous companion. Nursing did not interest her in the least— there were plenty of others to do it anyway—but her organisation was good.

Before 1914 there was little nursing done at the Hindu Rao, it being less of a real hospital than a show place of British administration in India. All this changed gradually as the war came raging over Europe, Asia and Africa, though it was not until the monsoon season of 1914-15 that we woke to the reality of war, and not till April was it realised that Australia was taking part in it. Then how I longed to get away and join the Sisters of the A.I.F. but it was not to be. Instead I nursed in India.

A sister was not supposed to demean herself by actually sponging and feeding patients and I was told I had lost face by personally caring for some wretched man in his extremity.

When General Sir Robert Scallon, Commander of all military forces in the Punjab, was smitten with septicaemia while riding from the frontier to take command in Mesopotamia he was brought to the Hindu Rao. Ministered to by scores of hands all day, he was supposed, when tucked up for the night, to sleep till morning. He didn't. Petulantly tossing and turning, he pushed the night orderly away, telling him to get out and stay out. Not knowing what to do, the attendant came to me.

The General was as grateful for my ministrations as the lion whose thorn was removed by the mouse, and when he went into a coma his A.D.C., Captain Raymond Daniels, told me the General's car and second charger were at my disposal, and mine only.

When he recovered, the General, before going on sick leave, advised the authorities in Simla to put me in charge of the hospital when Miss Dalrymple left to marry Captain Daniels. This far from pleased the lynx-eyed sisters, though naturally it astonished and gratified Miss Skinner.

The war was now raging and the sea full of danger from submarines and raiders, so, because there was nowhere else to send them, one or two maternity cases, prevented from going Home, came in to us.

Although Lady Minto was absent, the Viceroy and his teen-aged daughter, Diamond, were at the Lodge, and the grounds were covered with Kedah's tents for high-placed visitors. One of these was Mrs Sarrel, the Helen of Troy of India, who, taken ill and needing immediate surgery, was brought to the Hindu Rao. The Viceroy's physician performed the operation and every medical officer in Delhi was anxious to be at her service. It's hard to explain this lovely woman's charm and magnetism. She was like a white rose—not young, for her hair was white, nor was she old or would she be ever. The Viceroy sent her a clothes basket of flowers every day and her meals were brought from the Lodge in a hot water container. It was all one could do to drive doctors from her bedside, or high-placed officials from her room when they came to pay their respects. Her husband knelt in his mess kit all night by her bed after the crisis. Young officers begged to be allowed to 'just look at her for a minute'. A Begum like a white sugar loaf arrived, guarded by flunkeys in scarlet, and demanded admittance. Inside the room she removed her purdah and flopped in her jewelled cloth of gold robe at the patient's feet.

The Duke and Duchess of Suffolk were sitting with the patient after the operation, when she collapsed. Messengers scattered in all directions to find a doctor and as sometimes in emergency, none could be found. I, with the help of one of the English sisters who was scared to touch the precious lady, hove in and saved her life.

For this I gained much undeserved merit, and Mrs Sarrel could not bear me out of her sight. In fact, she wanted to take me away with her to Simla and attach me to herself for all time. The Devil tempted me, for she promised 'ways of pleasantness and paths of peace' but although attracted—as who was not?—by her beauty and magnetic charm, I did not really love her. I had my job to do and enjoyed doing it, so hugging my pride in conquering temptation, I declined her offer. Besides, I wanted to go back to Australia.

The cool season in Delhi that year was a triumphant time for me. Even as the hot season approached, and the Viceroy and entourage moved back to Simla and most of the ladies to the Hills to escape the heat, I still had a wonderful time. I was asked to all functions, cars were sent for me, generals opening the doors, colonels escorting me, majors shouting me cocktails at the Club, captains lending me their horses to ride, simply because I had nursed their brothers, wives and children. Even the Commissioner, Mr Hailey, dubbed 'Hail Hail Hail Lord God Almighty', asked me to a dinner party, taking me in as first lady—to my horror, for I didn't know what to talk to him about, or what to say to the archaeologist on the other side, or what to drink (for I dislike wine) or when to rise and nod to the other ladies to withdraw to the drawing-room. However, my chief swain, the officer in charge of the C.I.D. and an expert in tactics, was there and tipped me off.

The English soldiers now quartered in Delhi could not stand up to the heat and several died in the Fort Hospital. Lord Radnor, their colonel, therefore gained permission to have any placed on the danger list sent to the Hindu Rao.

The first to come was a huge sergeant dressed in layers of woollen garments—dressing-gown, pyjamas and what used to be called 'flannels'—and his temperature was dangerously high. 'Desperate remedies,' I grimaced, putting the stripped body under a wet sheet, with a fan blowing on it.

He had a great heart, that sergeant, but not a great head. He never slept and, his eyes wide open and wild, he defied medicine, food and drink. Two orderlies always sat by and two more helped to hold him when given food and medicine. At last his M.O. brought in three capsules, saying, 'If these don't make him sleep it's all up with him.'

A babe is hard enough to make swallow when it resists, but just you try it when the subject is of the 'Kiss me goodnight, sergeant-major' type! After the second dose the four orderlies and myself shook our heads and gave up.

In the morning the head bearer brought him egg and milk in a spouted feeding cup.

'Take it away, Lahorie,' I told him. 'It's no use trying any more.'

'Miss sahib, no one die while you nurse them,' he said and sat down cross-legged like an image, clutching the tray.

I went again to the bedside of the dying sergeant. His pulse was short and feeble, his skin wet and cold, his filmed eyes staring, his chin dropped. Lahorie now at my elbow shoved the cup into my hand and I put the capsule in the open mouth and the spout of the cup between the patient's strong white teeth.

The wrath of a roped panther was not to be compared to this dying Samson's fury. He roared, gargled, choked, as he struggled against the four orderlies. And then he bit the spout from the cup and spewed the egg and milk in his mouth all over me.

Lahorie hid his face. His miss sahib had been polluted.

But when I came forth cleansed, he met me with a complacent utterance. 'That ghora log fellah, he sleep. He get well now.'

The prophecy was fulfilled and before going on leave a friend brought the sergeant to say goodbye, both in full uniform. Saluting, the sergeant turned away, and his friend remonstrated, 'Ye never said nuffin' like y' said y' would say, sarge. Why didn't cher?'

''Cos I should've croid,' he said.

15

The Gilded Cage

All during that season of 1915-16 riots and insurrections went on around us. They are history now but horrifying to have lived through, though I had no sense of personal danger. One day Lahorie, my devoted bearer, had looked at me strangely and pointing to a mark of some kind that had appeared on my forehead, said, 'No native harm you, Miss Sahib, you have the holy mark.' In India things like that take on a special significance and I felt a certain reassurance in his assertion.

That was odd, but odder still was that one day a fakir crossed my path and squatted at my feet, though I told him to go away and that I had nothing to give him. 'No matter,' he said and drawing a circle in the dust wrote 'Danger'.

'What do you mean, Holy One?' I asked.

'Go from the city. Go far away, Miss Sahib. You die if you do not go. Enemy with green eye kill you.'

I gave him a rupee, for he seemed to be humble and sincere, sent him away and thought no more about it, though I later believed that the green eye to which he referred was jealousy and that thought waves for good or ill carry as surely as those of light or sound. From that time on I developed mysterious bouts of fever and had to take to my bed. It was from the behaviour and caustic comments of my relieving sister that I came to realise the hostility towards me of those who believed they had prior claims to my position. She received my callers or enquirers in such a way that they took an immediate dislike to her and she missed out on the invitations that were usually showered on nursing sisters. For this she blamed me, which made my life most unpleasant. It was with some relief, therefore, that when sufficiently recovered, I packed my bags to return to Australia on sick leave.

Everyone was by this time singing the praises of the Australian troops. 'The best soldiers that ever went to war,' it was said, '. . . only to be compared with the armies of old Rome and even resemble them in bearing, courage and physique.'

Mrs Highcome, the wife of a British officer, whom I had met casually in Delhi, decided at the last minute that instead of going to the hills for the summer she would come to Australia with me and meet some of these much lauded soldiers. She had never thought of Australia or Australians in her life before and had now formed some totally unreal impressions of both.

I, as a colonel's daughter and niece of other highly-placed army officials, was socially acceptable according to the standards of her kind and she seemed to have the idea of staying with my family at Applecross.

As we approached the wharf at Fremantle I, with my poor sight, asked her whether she saw anyone looking like my relatives.

'Certainly not,' she replied, 'but there's an old apple woman down there who appears to be waving to you with an umbrella, and there's some fellow beside her—a corporal I should say—with a bandaged face.'

'That apple woman,' I told her, as we came alongside the wharf, 'is my mother, and the corporal is my brother Jack who was wounded at Gallipoli.'

It was the first time it had struck me that Mother had aged and was no longer the smartly dressed leader of Perth society. The Australian sun, worry over her family and her beloved Bob who had been posted 'missing' in France, and the constant struggle to make ends meet had all taken their toll.

Mrs Highcombe decided she would not come home with us after all and, casting one horrified look around Fremantle, asked where anyone who was anyone stayed in this extraordinary place. We took her to the Palace Hotel, where I ran into the embrace of Deborah (now Lady) Hackett. Mrs Highcombe brightened a little on being introduced to her but Deb quickly wiped her off as an insufferable snob. She returned to India on the next ship to spread the news that Delhi's pet canary was nothing but a mudlark.

Soon after my return I tried to cut my contract with Lady Minto's and join the A.I.F. but with many applicants before me I had no hope of getting in for months. Then came a cable from the Minto Service in Calcutta ordering me to Burma, so off I sailed once more. While in Burma I finished a book I had started some time before which I called *Letters of a V.A.D.* This I gave to the writer Joseph Clayton (author of *The Times Encyclopaedia*'s 'History of Religion' and a biography of Father Staunton) whom I met at this time and who took it to London and arranged for its publication with Andrew Melrose & Co. Production was held up by the wartime shortage of paper and when it eventually saw the light war books were no longer in much demand.

Finding it impossible to join the A.I.F. I had before leaving Australia applied to join the Queen Alexandra Military Nursing Service and while in Burma received word that my application had been accepted. I was posted to Bombay to nurse in the palace of the Maharajah Geckwar of Baroda which had been given over to the authorities as a hospital for officers. The patients called it 'The Gilded Cage' and this bird at least was miserable there.

The Sisters' Club was a small palace and since no one was allowed to die on the Rajah's premises lest his spirit put a hoodoo on them, no one seriously ill was admitted to the hospital.

There were just enough certificated nurses to cover each ward, the rest of the nursing staff being V.A.D's, mostly charming grass widows, dressed as we were in plain white but with their veils knotted at the back. Their pay was only a fraction less than ours and as often as not they would hand their cheques with a laugh to the nearest orderly.

Miss Lamb, the sister in charge, beribboned in her scarlet cape and facings, decided that Miss Skinner and her friend, Miss Henderson, both being the products of some second-rate and outdated London training, must be 'put in their place'. Henderson was one of the first of the New Women. She made it her business to join as an auxiliary every corps for the required six months, and now wore ribbons for France and Egypt as well as the Serbian Ivory Cross. Her next objective was Mesopotamia.

Miss Lamb dealt with me by putting me as the only nurse on perpetual night duty. How I longed for home during those long night watches, the patients as I walked the huge wards sleeping like so many exhibition models under smoothed sheets. I would sit in the trellised marble verandahs watching the misty moon and stars, my ears buzzing with the noise of mosquitoes and the effects of quinine.

At last Henderson, equally depressed, demanded of head office that we both transferred to Mespot, but we were told that we were too useful where we were.

'We'll have to jump it,' said Henderson, and jump it she did, though on her own and through her own ingenuity.

Henderson was in charge of the meanest ward—the Ear, Nose and Throat, Gastric and Observation Cases, to which no one seriously disabled was ever admitted, but hearing of the imminent visit of the new Viceroy with the General in Charge of the Medical Corps, she made it her job to see that her patients looked impressive. A patient with nothing more serious than nose-bleeding was put in a back-splint, another recovering from a camel's bite was put under an iron cradle. A gastric case was given crutches and his leg put in plaster. All the rest were bandaged, one with sticking plaster all over his head and face.

When his excellency appeared with the medico general the innocent victims, bursting with suppressed delight, played their parts nobly. Miss Lamb and the colonel in charge of the hospital, who followed the entourage, nearly collapsed at the sight that met their eyes but could do nothing about it. The Viceroy paused compassionately before the man with the bandaged face, took his hand and glanced with admiration at Henderson.

She had made the impression she intended and was sent to Mesopotamia.

One day in town, when trying in vain to book a passage for Australia, I encountered a certain V.A.D. from the Gilded Cage. She was young, glamorous and high born—a charming witch. She asked why I looked so dejected and when I told her my tale of woe she smiled mysteriously: 'Cheer up, Sister,' she said, 'Leave it to me.'

Soon afterwards I was transferred to an enormous hospital at Mhaw where the wards were packed with men from France who were too sick to fight but too precious to disband in England. But my homesickness was now almost past bearing.

Then the magic happened. Called to the office to face an angry Chief M.O. I was asked how I dared go behind their backs to get a transfer arranged for me to Australia.

I was as astonished as they had been to see on the table before them orders and passes for Sister Skinner to travel first class from Mhaw to Bombay, Bombay to Madras, Madras to Colombo, and there to await transport at government expense for Australia.

The witch had waved her broomstick.

16

Home

I did not get back to join the A.I.F. until late in 1917. It was too late to be sent overseas, but how I loved them all at the Base Hospital. How generous, happy and free from petty snobbery were our Australian sisters; how gallant, merry and uncomplaining our boys.

While in quarantine nursing the men brought back with pneumonic influenza I wrote articles for *The West Australian* and earned high praise and I again thought I might yet become a recognised writer, but it was only a flash in the pan.

Still, what mattered to me most of all was that I was home again. The Hand had pushed me into pleasant places—but I could never have settled there. Not on your life! I was a roving soldier's daughter on one side and a shellback on the other. Paradoxical to a degree, though I loved the traditional code, the sweeping offhand manners of the insular English, I rejoiced in the carefree capability of the Australians, not only of the returned men but the rejects who while 'the boys' were at the war had completed the railway across the thousand miles of desert dividing east from west and husbanded the sheep until wool sales attended by foreign buyers could again be held.

Western Australia, occupied for less than a century, not twenty years a State, had been bereft of most of its manpower for three years. The goldfields were deserted, the huge wheat and sheep properties neglected, the dairying and timber industries just holding together, women keeping the home fires burning on the scattered properties. The cry was now 'back to the land', and the boys, many of them shattered in body and mind, exchanged their battle-stained uniforms for dungarees and old felt hats.

I too felt the call of the land and when asked to take over a hospital at Jardee, one of the south-western timber-milling towns,

I jumped at it. How different the life here from that I had lived in England and India—and how I loved it! This south-western corner had a special attraction for me, perhaps because my grandfather had been one of the first to attempt to ship timber from that area. Walking in the forest as I did during my time off, I would picture him strutting about, thumbs in the armholes of his yellow waistcoat, sizing up the enormous boles of jarrah; hear the eloquence with which he extolled the potential wealth these trees represented to the colony and argued with the masters of the sailing ships under contract to load the first shipments for the English market. They had put their thumbs in their belts and told him straight: 'Ain't in the charter, yer ludship. We can't load logs what's bigger than the *Saucy Ann* herself.' Grandfather lost that argument and his venture came to grief.

During my time at Jardee I came to know and admire the forestry men of the south-west. They dedicated their lives to those forests and were as hardy, courageous and self-sacrificing as the men in charge of the sailing ships of earlier days. Day after day they would wend their separate ways through the mighty ranks of that brooding, arrogant timber, watching for its enemies, marking its weaker specimens. They built their watchtowers like crows' nests atop the highest trees and there sat alert through the heat of the summer to spot the first sign of a forest fire. I never heard them complain of the loneliness, though their only companions were the quiet hawks, screeching parrots, inquisitive possums, and bees seeking nectar from the gum blossoms.

I grew to love also the rough humanity of the timber workers, and learnt to know the inherent stamina, fortitude and joyful courage of the outback women from the little holdings, orchards and dairies of the cleared areas. These women came in to Jardee to have their babies, travelling by cart over miles and miles of winding forest tracks, often alone and at night with no light but a kerosene hurricane lantern, and no companion but an old grey mare. What courage to face the ghostly shadows and eerie sounds of the dark bush! What temerity to live closed in by miles of jarrah forest away from human help and companionship! What fortitude to carry on with the milking, the weeding, the care of poultry and pigs while 'hubby' went off with his bullock team to earn wages hauling logs, clearing, fencing, wellsinking and house-building! What stamina to bear and rear children under circumstances such as theirs!

When the tobacco and dairy industries developed around Manjimup that town became the main centre for the district, but when I arrived Jardee was considered the coming place, the railway from Perth running out through Katanning and Bridgetown and thence through the lonely forest to the little town. It consisted of a group of small timber houses, including the doctor's and mill manager's residences and the mill itself. It had no hotel apart from a hostel attached to a canvas encampment. I did not realise at the time that Katherine Susannah Prichard was then staying in this camp, writing *Working Bullocks* and absorbing the atmosphere of the forests and the life of its people of which she wrote so vividly. I was not to meet her until later for my life at that time was completely centred around the hospital.

My staff consisted of one other nurse, an orderly and a maid. Fred the orderly was the general factotum, keeping the floors at a high polish, milking the cows, chopping the wood, helping to nurse the men and assisting at post mortems. He did not care what he did so long as he could continue to bet on horses running on faraway race-courses. There was no radio then but he followed his fancy horses and jockeys through the newspapers. Lizzie the cook was much of a feather and I fancy they 'spliced up' later.

The medical officer—always called Rupert behind his back—was the only doctor for many miles around. Calvinistic, cold, implacable and arrogant, he was not an attractive character. Trusting no one, he supervised every detail of hospital administration. During the summer months he and he alone held the key to the water tanks and he would stand by while Fred filled the buckets, one for the cow, two for the kitchen, one for each ward. He made regular inspections of the kitchen and cupboards, weighed out all provisions and measured the medical stores—never neglecting to check the contents of the brandy bottle. He would not let the nurses do the dressings for the male patients, although they would have much preferred our ministrations to those of himself and Fred. He seemed to begrudge his patients the slightest pleasure. He forbade smoking or beer in the wards and if his patients craved meat he put them on farinaceous foods. Before his patients left the hospital, however—usually in a fairly weak and confused state—he presented them with the Entry and Discharge book and insisted on their writing under 'Remarks': 'I have no complaints to make.' He never laughed and joked with anyone and children took to their heels at sight of him. On Sundays he set up a tub and held services which no one attended except those physically unable to escape.

None-the-less he was a good doctor, a skilful and resourceful surgeon, often carrying out first rate operations under circumstances that most doctors would consider impossible. For this I admired him but his callousness often chilled me to the marrow. If, when acting as his anaesthetist, I became alarmed about a patient's condition, he would snap back at me: 'Carry on. It is I who have to face the coroner.'

Skilful in other respects he was, alas, no born accouchier. I was never allowed to deliver a baby, though I longed to do so, as none of his cases ever went straight. I don't know why, for he stuck to the rules. His touch just seemed somehow to upset the equilibrium. None of them succumbed, however, before the spring when a crisis occurred in his unpopular regime.

We had, during this season, a sudden and unaccountable influx of patients, such as every hospital has to contend with from time to time. Besides accidents, pneumonia and maternity cases there was an old Chinese man suffering from a stroke. And then scarlet fever broke out. The isolation ward was opened and my nurse took charge of it, Gertrude, the doctor's sister-in-law, a partly trained nurse, taking her place beside me. Gertrude was a pink and white Tasmanian girl with a cynical turn of mind, amused by everything, particularly by the martinet Rupert whom, though she was obliged in the circumstances to obey, she neither loved nor honoured.

We were working in high gear, the maternity ward full, and besides all the other cases an irascible consumptive with a weak heart in the throes of acute pneumonia, when Rupert sent in a patient for abdominal surgery. I pleaded with him to put it off while the scarlet fever was at its height and we were so short-handed but he was adamant.

'The wardsmaid can look after the women and the orderly the men,' he said. 'Gertrude can take over the anaesthetic after the patient is under and you can assist me.'

The oracle had spoken. We had a day to organise while he went off on his regular visit to Big Brook, returning with a Mrs Evans who had booked in for confinement two months later. She was sickening for scarlet fever so I put her in the only empty ward and cared for her apart from the others. Her baby was born dead before nightfall and she followed it a few hours later. Upset and scared to the marrow about the general situation, I begged Rupert once more to defer the operation but he merely ordered me to soak in a disinfectant bath and carry on.

During my last round that night I found the other patients upset too, for it had been impossible to keep them in ignorance of the day's fatalities.

'Poor old Evans,' one of the timber workers muttered, 'his missus gone like that and six little kids under ten.'

'Two deaths!' another exploded. 'There's got to be a third.'

'There'll be nothing of the sort,' I snorted, but seeing the Reaper with his scythe around every corner as I completed my rounds.

Joy cometh in the morning! Mrs Lyall, the mill manager's charming wife, one of the Bussell family from Busselton, had organised a busy bee to look after the hospital during the operation, though how she had realised our dilemma I have no idea.

The operation was nearly over and a complete success, when Mrs Lyall knocked on the door and brought in one of the precious babies, haemorrhaging after circumcision and in its last extremities.

In ten days the hospital was empty except for the Chinese patient suffering from a stroke. Rumours of the doctor's neglect spread like wildfire and Rupert closed the hospital doors while the rumpus raged. It was a distressing situation. The secretary of the Road Board requested us not to leave until things had straightened out but when the nurse gave notice the doctor decided to send the remaining patient down to Perth. It was nobody's fault that the man was at death's door, but Rupert knew that the loss of yet another of his patients would be disastrous at this stage. There was no one to accompany him but myself and I sat on a packing case beside him in the luggage van. It was the funniest journey of my life, for at Bridgetown the van was filled with carcases of pigs hung from hooks in the roof. I didn't mind. It was a typical Australian journey.

After my return to Jardee I became very friendly with the Lyalls, splendid people who enjoyed the kindly fruits of the earth and loved their neighbours as themselves. But because of rather than in spite of this fact, Rupert disliked them intensely. Poor Rupert! He had now not only no friends, as before, but many enemies. His wife became seriously ill and her sister Gertrude took her back to Tasmania, but Rupert, sticking against all opposition to the terms of his contract, held on.

During this time he was called on to perform a post mortem on a former patient at the hospital—the irascible consumptive with the weak heart. It seemed that the old fellow was always grizzling and complaining to his wife and fifteen-year-old son and that the boy had one day picked up a brick and threatened to throw it at him if he continued scolding his long-suffering mother. The man had jumped from his chair in a rage and fallen dead in the doorway. Rupert's finding was that he had died of heart failure caused by the criminal actions of the son, who was forthwith arrested for manslaughter.

The mill hands were so enraged at this that the managers decided to call a meeting, giving Rupert a chance to reply to their complaints about himself.

When ex-patients aired their grouches about the hospital he pointed to their signatures to the statement that they had no complaints to make. When accused of negligence or carelessness he declared that he was ready to face the court if they were prepared to prove it. Finally he was asked why, during his term of office, no staff had remained more than a few months at the hospital. To this he replied that any deaths or disasters that had occurred there had been the fault of incompetent nurses, particularly matrons, who had been capable only of unlocking the Golden Gates.

'The war has so depleted the country of capable nurses,' he declared, 'that the only ones available are negligent, ignorant and inefficient. Some, in fact, are nothing but drunken strumpets.'

Everyone gasped with indignation and up stood a timid little shell-shocked soldier called Jock whom I had nursed at the Base. He had been nearly demented at that time, the sound of a tray falling being enough to make him cling in terror to the bedpost. I had been able to laugh him out of it and for this he was pathetically grateful.

'Tak' back yon lie if ye be alluding to Sister Skinner,' he shouted. 'She's no inefficient, no negligent, and she never unlocked no golden gates.'

Rupert looked at him and drawled: 'And what is Sister Skinner to you, Jock MacPherson?'

The little soldier sank back, terrified that to say any more might be to compromise us both.

I had stayed on at Jardee in the belief that Rupert must surely make his departure before long, but now it seemed there would be no shifting him until his contract had expired. After that meeting the hospital staff walked out with me at their head and I went home to Mother.

17

D. H. Lawrence at Darlington

When I left Jardee something that wanted to be free and 'gang m' ain gait' broke out in me. All I wanted was to sit down with my feet in the bush and drink tea from the family billy.

Jack had been granted, under the Returned Soldiers' Settlement Scheme, a small farm at Kalamunda in the hills near Perth. He also received a pension of ten shillings a week and a double set of teeth which, when in his mouth, he could only clench. There was a little orchard on the property, a pig and a cow or two and a cabbage patch.

Estelle, Dollie and Nazeli were now married and away, Bob still on the 'missing' list and little hope now left of his ever being seen again,* so Mother sold the Applecross home and put up a little cottage next door to Jack's farm and moved in with Mittie.

Mother's income was less than 300 pounds a year but she now wanted nothing more. She was content to sit in her cottage like a deposed queen, and when her rich relations visited, to give them baskets of Jack's cabbages and oranges. Mittie had nothing except what Mother allowed her but I, having been brought up in Scotland to 'tak' care o' the pence and the pounds'll tak care o' themselves', had saved almost all my pay since returning from India, and could afford to do nothing for a while.

I soon found, however, that I wasn't in the least free or 'ganging m' ain gait', so I donned the old uniform, took a house in the township and opened it as a convalescent home. It quickly filled and although it meant hard work I was making out quite well with Jack providing cabbages and Mittie butter, cream and eggs.

Then it looked like a crash for me because the owner of the house wanted to sell it and gave notice of eviction.

Thank God for the gift of friendship. A Quaker nurse, Miss

* Bob was eventually reported 'Killed in action'.

Nellie Beakbane, convalescing in my wobbling establishment, offered partnership, on equal terms in return for my good will. A place called Leithdale at Darlington was on the market, and there we moved.

The family immediately came to Darlington too, Jack exchanging his farm at Kalamunda for an unstocked three acres by the brook. He moved Mother's cottage and re-erected it beside a four-roomed dwelling already there.

In our establishment Nellie ran the house with a cook and house-maid and I, with the help of an old Irishman named Martin, ran the outside, did the washing-up and the household washing for which Martin drew the water, lit the copper fire and turned the mangle. His brogue was still on him, though he had previously been turning a windlass for fifty years on the goldfields, and he was happy to be at Darlington to end his days. Here he could grow things in the damp rich ground, milk the cow and drive the old horse and phaeton to meet guests at the station, bring them over the brook and up the steepest bit of 'the worst cow of a hill in Western Australia' and point out at the top the glorious view.

That's how it was—all settled in—until in May 1922 Mrs Jenkins ('Pussy' to her friends) rang to ask if we could 'accommodate' (hateful word) her shipboard acquaintances, Mr and Mrs D. H. Lawrence, he a famous writer and she a German countess.*

Inwardly I rebelled. Why should I chore for a famous author and his high-falutin' wife whom Pussy, with her glamour and charm, had taken under her wing? (I couldn't stand Pussy at that stage, though later I found her rather sweet.) But remembering my 'good will' against my partner's thousands, I told her we had a nice double room in the front of the house, and that the Eustace Cohens were staying with us and they would probably all get on well.

* 'Pussy' Jenkins: Mrs A. L. Jenkins (née Burt), a member of one of Western Australia's most prominent families, met the Lawrences on board the *Oronsay* in February 1922 when they were travelling from Naples to Ceylon. H. E. L. Priday of W.A. Newspapers Limited, describes her thus:

> Mrs Jenkins . . . was a travelled woman with outspoken and mature views unclouded by sentiment. . . . One was at once captivated by her rich and racily humorous personality. She liked talking and I am sure that D. H. Lawrence liked listening to her. It is evident from their subsequent exchange of letters that both he and his wife enjoyed her company and appreciated the services she was able to do for them in Australia. How much they really liked her is evident from their subsequent invitation to go to Mexico with them.

Edward Nehls: *D. H. Lawrence, A Composite Biography*, Vol. II, p. 116.

The maid being out when they arrived, I took tea to them on the verandah and I recall my annoyance when Pussy, with one of her amused, sidelong glances, shoved a bag of cakes into my hands.

I wondered which of the two handsome fellows in the party was the author, for surely the frail little red-bearded man whom Pussy was gushing over could not be he.

But of course it was.

The Lawrences, though a little aloof, showed that the place pleased them, and that they liked the Cohens too, Eustace being a brilliant artist and musician and Maudie, lately his bride, delightful, handsome and vivacious. We put them all at the same table and as I knew Maudie very well she would regale me with snippets of their dinner-time talk.

A school teacher then holidaying with us had lent her Lawrence's *The White Peacock* with a warning about some of his other books such as *Sons and Lovers, Aaron's Rod* and *The Rainbow,* adding sotto voce 'He writes about *sex*'. Maudie told me she didn't believe it as she had found Lawrence so polite, amusing and kind. She read *The White Peacock,* didn't think much of it and told him so. Furthermore she said that Mollie Skinner had written one just as good which she would lend him so that he could see for himself. He accepted the offer and read *Letters of a V.A.D.*

A surprise for Mrs Lawrence who found Nellie and said, 'But how stupid you people are! You do not know my husband. He is the genius Lawrence, and this man who startles his contemporaries and makes them wild because they cannot write so well as he does, walks up and down the verandah with Miss Skinner's book and says "It is good—so good." He wants to talk to her. She does not give him the chance. How absurd this is! Why does she not talk to him?'

'Because she has her work to do,' said my Quaker friend, unperturbed. 'If he wants to talk to her I expect he'll find her in the wash-house.'

Which he did, bringing his shipboard white socks to wash himself, because someone he was fond of had knitted them for him. The socks on the line, he sat on the bench and watched old Martin with his gnarled hands on the handle of the mangle, ignoring his presence completely. As Martin went off, Lawrence looked after the sturdy old chap with his frayed clothes, bent back and crooked legs but still unyielding to age.

It was then I noticed those wonderful eyes. They were flecked with colours, changing like a chameleon with his changing moods and at all times filled with light. Now they were full of love for his brother man, and I forgot his frailty, his beard, his scarlet lips and the hectic flush on the cheekbones of his otherwise white face. He gave out courage.

Picking up a lump of the gum that oozed from the cracks of a huge redgum by the stable, he brought it over to me.

'This tree seems to sweat blood,' he remarked. 'A hard dark blood of agony. It frightens me—all the bush out beyond stretching away over these hills frightens me, as if dark gods possessed the place. My very soul shakes with terror when I wander out there in the moonlight.'

'We see you from our beds on the back verandah,' I said, 'and wish you would not go. You might easily get lost—which would be frightening enough, dark gods or not.'

'I shall go, as long as I stay here,' he said. 'Do you hear the kangaroos calling softly when everything is still? Roo! Roo! Roo!'

'It's odd, but I do, and odder still that you do. People say it's my imagination, that roos don't call, but they'll admit that emus do. They make a drumming mysterious sound that frightens the guts out of new chums, up north.' Half chagrined that he had drawn me out and half responding to an invisible wire that linked us I went on. 'Of course it's ridiculous, but I also hear on a still night sounds like band music—orchestral music I don't recognise. It's absurd, for there's no band within miles of us.'

'Why don't you write about this strange country?' he said. 'About how it was met by the first settlers?'

Not answering, I hung the sheets on the line and while they flapped in the sunshine against the blue sky, a muscovy duck brought her brood round the wash-house. They were golden globs and she white as snow, looking beautiful because she was angry and ruffled. She stamped her feet, hissing (muscovies don't quack) and the ducklings sat down and there she left them, disappearing the way she had come. The ducklings sat on, snapping at insects. Lawrence shooed them to go after her but they refused to move. He looked at me, his eyebrows raised, and presently a poor little tired one appeared, the mother duck driving it to join its fellows.

'She must have gone back for it,' Lawrence said, as they all moved off, and added, 'I asked you why you don't write about the early settlers. A Mr Siebenhaur brought me his poems to read, and—much more interesting—a little year book, a kind of diary of events from the foundation of the colony till it became a State. You should write of it. I would if I stayed. The settlers—men and women with their children arriving here, dumped on the sand with the surf behind them, a few merchants, a few soldiers, a few packing cases into which they crept for shelter after chucking out the pianos; building camp ovens, burning their hands, looking for fresh water, longing for achievement, hungry for land, their cattle starving, their women scolding, homesick but full of courage, courage carrying them forward. What kept them here?'

As he spoke there was magic in the air. We sat in civilization, near a great pittosporum tree covered with blossom; beyond lay the orange orchard with its golden blobs of fruit. And just over the fence the summer bush crouched down, acrid and harsh, with great granite rocks thrusting between prickly shrubs.

'You have only seen the bush at its worst,' I said. 'If you go East, try and come this way in September after the winter rains.' I told him how the trees took on a new look in the spring, how their leaves danced in the sunlight and the saplings looked more like youth personified than ghosts; how the harshest looking bushes were covered with blossom, the ground was scattered with our unique and lovely wildflowers. I described the satiny white bridal creeper and glowing pink coral creeper that covered the fallen logs and blasted tree trunks, the delicate orchids that cropped up everywhere, and best of all the leschenaultia like fragments of blue sky tossed down to earth by angels.

He said nothing and, feeling a fool, I walked with him down to the house.

But later Nellie Beakbane said Frieda, as we called the countess behind her back, had been raving on at her about my 'stupidity' (which, incidentally, my partner, not liking the idea of my efforts to write, thoroughly approved of), and about her adored Lorenzo's interest in me. She couldn't understand it, because he was usually so 'difficult', whereas here at Leithdale both he and she were very happy.

This encouraged me to give Lawrence the script of *Black Swans* and when he had read it we had many conversations while everyone else was lying down after lunch. They were engineered by Frieda with her unconcerned laugh, though that she was not unconcerned I later heard from my Quaker friend with whom she hit it off so well. The whole thing was odd—paradoxical.

Since then I have often wished that there had been a dictaphone to record what Lawrence, so misunderstood in his day, said to me. He revealed himself as a man of great spiritual integrity who had not discarded the long long thoughts of boyhood—nor a boy's wilfulness and explosive fits of temper and defiance of authority. When punished, he would take it, cocky when done with. When he knew he was right, he would show he was right. He wanted to be understood, to be loved, but he was going to play with fire even if it burnt his fingers. It didn't matter to him who else got burnt, that wasn't his affair. And there, puzzled, I sat and listened to him, this man-boy with the little red beard, scarlet lips, strange eyes flashing with amused lights, and an upright frail body held with dignity.

I came to see that the man I had thought so inconspicuous was beautiful—hardly a man, but a spirit, unfinished, like music. I felt a piercing sorrow for him—a child locked out with a burden of grief. I would always know he was not a sensual man but a creature of fire. Whatever he said, or did, or wrote I would understand him. But I did not love him. I could not bear to be with him for long for he scorched and seared my spirit.

'You are going to write that book about the settlers, eh?' he kept urging. 'Put *Black Swans* aside. Take the new book from the time when you became aware of what went on in this empty country. Know your characters, strip them to the bone. Away with fancy and sentiment, be spiteful. Who do you know for a hero?'

Then my brother Jack passed and I nodded towards him. Sapped of vitality by his wounds, he still moved with easy grace, his damaged head held high, and he gave out to me at least the music of humour and courage.

Though Lawrence had not met Jack, he knew him somehow, though Jack for his part had asked me who the 'Creeping Jesus' was he had seen mooching around the bush. Jack's question is not surprising (though neither Jesus nor Lawrence ever crept) for Lawrence had something about him that artists paint when visualising Jesus. It was something of the inward strength that comes from purpose, and of the yearning and sadness that comes from loving where love is spurned. Perhaps Lawrence himself was aware of this and in his egotism thought he could walk on equal terms with God and Satan too, linking them hand in hand (Oh! that lovely story of his about Jesus walking in the tomb, so exquisitely told—and then turning that triumph over to the Devil).

Not that he showed anything but the kindness in him when at

Leithdale. When asking me to write this book about the settlers he made me think of the flame that springs up when the sun sinks in the clear atmosphere of the wide empty spaces.

When he looked at Jack I knew that he saw hidden under that sagging old army uniform the heart of my brother, the do-or-die in him. 'Make your brother your hero,' he said. 'I don't like that sort of man myself—*giving* himself for his country. The stupidity of war! But he is the ideal framework for your boy in the bush. You love him and watch him—you know how he reacts.'

I protested that to write of those I knew intimately would bring hell's fire on my head; that I could not bear not to be loved by those about me; that everything I wrote made them scoff, which was why the V.A.D. was published under a nom-de-plume; that I was scared of writing what went on about me. I said that why I had not developed an individual style was because I had so little education on account of the eye trouble that had kept me for so long in a dark room, and that although I was a good midwife I was unsure of myself as a writer.

'I'm so poor it's dangerous,' I told him. 'I can't climb mountains. I'm not educated, but I can keep myself and it leaves me little time to write.'

'But you're not always so busy here. You could sit down at a certain hour, morning or evening.'

'What about the story?'

'You need no story.'

'Construction?'

'You need none.' (Later he bitterly condemned me for lack of it.)

'I have no time.'

'You can take an hour—the same hour—that's very important—daily. Write bit by bit of the scenes you have witnessed, the people you know, describing their reactions as you know they do react, not as you imagine they should. You spoil things by rewriting. Write and build up from day to day.'*

* Why did Lawrence give Mollie Skinner this advice? Most of her work suffered from lack of revision, as he must have realised. His friend, Henry James Foreman, quotes him as having said in about 1921:

> I write every book three times. By that I don't mean copying and revising as I go along, but literally. After I finish the first draft I put it aside and write another. Then I put the second aside and a write a third.

Edward Nehls, *D. H. Lawrence, A Composite Biography*, Vol. II, University of Wisconsin Press, 1958, p. 106.

'And what about the end?'

'When you've done 80,000 words, throw down your pen.'

'I've no style,' I hedged.

'Style!' he snorted. 'What is it? You have been given the Divine Spark and would bury it in a napkin!' He was gazing at the orange trees, the sun shining silver on the polished leaves, the fruit golden, and the heavy blossom sweet on the air.

Presently he said more gently, 'Read the European writers, learn how they do it. You can't get hold of translations? Well, write as you do, simply. Write when the passion is upon you, expunge later, and away with anyone's feelings—they won't recognise themselves when they read it, so why worry? And don't be sentimental.'

His scorn, his contempt for the sentimental and 'fancy' as he called it, that he had found in me was somehow mixed with sorrow and tenderness, and feeling embarrassed I got up, saying, 'If I wrote this book, who would publish it?'

'Send it to me,' he said. 'I'll look after that.'

At other times he told of his nostalgia for England and Europe, but said he wouldn't go back until he had seen more of Australia, which had already fascinated and at the same time frustrated him.

'We may go to Mexico,' he said. 'A woman there has sent us a large cheque to visit her. I don't want to go, but probably will. I must see something of the world and travelling is expensive.' He laughed, full of mischief. 'I had a fiendish time fighting against the well-known writers to make good. They hate me, most of them—though we have marvellous friends amongst those who do not. Funds did not meet a lay-out to travel, so I went round with the hat. I was given a fiver and told to go back to school teaching. No matter. We are very happy here. Frieda wants to buy a little farm and stay here.'

The idea of the lovely Frieda cooking and washing and keeping the kitchen fire alight, and her husband, always so clean and well dressed, ploughing and feeding the pigs and chickens, made me laugh.

The funny thing about the Lawrences' stay at Leithdale was that they liked not being known as celebrities. The only person who knew that D.H. was a really great writer was Katherine Susannah Prichard (Mrs Hugo Throssell) who happened to be confined with her son Ric the night she heard he was at Leithdale. Captain Throssell came up from Greenmount in a great to-do to arrange a meeting. But it was not to be. The Lawrences went on before it could be managed.

18

Group Settlement

When the Lawrences had gone we thought little more about them. Our season had then been in full swing but with the onset of the November heat holidaymakers turned to the surf and sea breezes of the coast. Dry east winds swept in over the Darling Ranges and Leithdale more or less went to sleep. Nellie Beakbane did not mind the winds but the bushfires that sometimes came rollicking along with them almost sent her crazy.

One of the maids, Jenny Wren, adjusted herself magnificently to both of us. Her vernacular was priceless and her stories naughty. Nellie did not know how naughty they were, and what would she have said to this? 'I'm Mrs Wren really. You see, I hopped it over the Nullarbor from South Australia when I found out that my hubby was a great bully of a lumper, not the nice cove all dressed up, with a cigar, who led me to the altar. Fair jealous he was too and had the cheek to set a dick to watch me, and was he wild when he found me stroking the dick's mou! He knocked him flat and turned on me, so I scooted.'

As the heat of summer intensified my mind seemed to flare up like the dry bush. I remembered Lawrence and began the book he had suggested about the settlers. The family scoffed, saying it was not fair to Miss Beakbane, but she herself had by that time become interested in the idea.

The book, which I called 'The House of Ellis', was finished by the following March and badly typed as it was went off to its sponsor, by this time in Mexico.

Then Mother died.

In my case it was queer that I felt it so much, since I had never pleased her and our minds were not closely linked. But the fact remains, I wilted, and Nellie, dismayed at my suffering, arranged to let Leithdale and visit her people in England. I, in the meantime, was to live in Mother's cottage and look after the family affairs.

The Lawrences had been gone a year, distance made correspondence difficult, and I had almost forgotten them and the book.

I tried to content myself at home but Lord, I couldn't stand it. Hoping that manual work would assuage grief and that I would be able to finish my novel *Black Swans* I undertook to open a government hospital for migrants in the Margaret River district of the southwest.

In that year (1923) the Western Australian government had agreed to receive 6000 emigrant families from Great Britain under what was known as the Group Settlement Scheme—a project aimed to develop the backward south-west of the State while relieving England's growing economic pressure.

What a lone, lost corner of the bush this was—cut off behind Cape Leeuwin, the river unnavigable, the giant forest overpowering, the nearby coast rugged, magnificent and sometimes terrifying. For untold ages the waters of the Southern and Indian Oceans, meeting in fury and dashing on the headland, had caused mariners to flee, before, in 1802, Matthew Flinders had nosed his ship in on the south of the great head and found the bay that bears his name.

Actually the government hospital I opened was not in the Margaret River township but at Karridale, ten miles nearer Cape Leeuwin. A rough road ran from Busselton, through Margaret River and Karridale to the Leeuwin Head, while not long before a railway had been laid down and a twice-weekly train service established. Road and line met at Flinders and followed the coast to the Cape, giving magnificent views of the sea and forest and massive rock formations that bore down on it.

There had once been a mill at Karridale from which the sawn timber was transferred—God knows how and man has forgotten— to the sailing ships that then called at Flinders Bay. All that was now left of the mill was the late manager's fine residence, a tiny church, a hall and a barn. The house had been transformed into a hospital for the groupies, the barn into a post office of sorts and the hall renovated for social gatherings. Only the church remained untouched and here it was that Brother Charles, a High Church Anglican priest of the Bush Brotherhood and as handsome as a young saint in an abbey window, held monthly services.

So far the surrounding forest had given way very little to civilisation. Any impact the mill had made was now unnoticeable and the cleared areas where settlers had hewn out their little properties were few. No wonder the immigrants were bewildered on arriving to take over the hundred-acre allotments that had sounded, at home, like princely estates.

The great benefits bestowed by the government were pointed out. What with a new four-roomed timber house and dairy on each holding, stock on tick, all requests attended to by regular inspectors, free carriage of heavy goods by rail and truck, and a regular three quid a week to buy stores, the immigrants could surely see they were being spoonfed.

Often the poor immigrant men were bossed by their families, Ma sticking up for her kids right or wrong and Pa stumping off alone with his billy and tucker-bag to hack hopelessly at the stubborn forest, do a bit of burning off, then sit down to wipe his brow and go to sleep. But when he got home, he expected his dinner. 'Why can't yer chop the kindling in the day-toime, Ma, instead of me havin' to 'old the lantern for yer in the dark?'

The old settlers laughed at their helplessness, remembering the dauntless spirit with which their own forbears, though no less immigrants themselves, had met far greater odds.* They had not been defeated by the untamed forest, the inland cliffs, the caves and caverns discovered when seeking their wandering cattle; not by the eerie Blackwood River where treacherous logs lay decaying under the dark water, or even by the prickly scrub that lured their stock to destruction.

But those pioneers had been for the most part of British farming stock and had far more idea of what they were coming to and how to cope with it than had these products of the crowded industrial towns. Few of the 'groupies' knew anything about farming at all and the raw land daunted and frustrated them. It was also obvious, however, that the whole scheme had been too hastily and optimistically devised. The organisation was poor and the administration generally showed lack of experience and imagination. It can hardly

* In 1829 when Britain took possession of the west side of Australia, Captain John Molloy, with a handful of soldiers and artisans and four members of the Bussell family, was sent there to form a settlement. They came out on the *Warrior*, left Fremantle on the *Emily Taylor*, arriving at Flinders Bay in May 1830, and founded the settlement of Augusta at the mouth of the Blackwood.

be wondered at that the majority drifted away to more developed areas. Indirectly the scheme did benefit the State by bringing out a great number of immigrants who, even if they failed to develop the dairying industry, settled down eventually and produced Australian born families.

At the time of my arrival the drawbacks of the project were more apparent than the advantages but the need of those homesick and disappointed migrants aroused my instinct to heal and love. I found the job satisfying and often so absorbing that instead of sinking into apathy at my critical time of life, I felt rejuvenated.

The staff at my little hospital consisted of two nurses, a cook and an orderly. The district M.O. lived at Margaret River, a fair-sized township with a proper hospital. Sunday was his 'groupies' day so, contrary to the usual order, Sunday was our busiest time. The cook and the orderly, however, still insisted on making it their day of rest, leaving the kitchen to be over-run by mothers and babies.

Inside it was Hades, doctor pulling teeth, lancing boils, shouting for this and that, swearing joyfully, slapping mustard plasters on backs, painting snow-white bosoms with black iodine, plastering ulcerated legs with Unna's paste, excising tonsils without anaesthetic, putting stinging drops in eyes. How they loved it! How important to be bandaged! If Doc didn't have time they gleefully bandaged themselves. They understood doctors, even the old-fashioned colonial type. This one was a coper of considerable resource but, unlike that dour Calvinist Rupert, an apostle of joy.

Once an old woman who had fallen and put her hip out of joint was carried in on a gate. She was in agony and I rang the doctor, begging him to come at once. He said, 'Give her a shot of morphia, fill her up with brandy and bring her in to Margaret hospital. I'm operating, but I'll fix her as soon as possible.'

It was dreadful getting her into a car with that dangling limb and taking her over bumps and potholes on the ill-made road. The brandy soothed her somewhat, but it was an ordeal for everyone. All the way I thought dismally of old ladies I had seen crippled for life even when their dislocated hips had been immediately wired by skilful surgeons.

But doctor was far from dismal when he breezed in to see her. He ran his hand over the swollen seat of injury, told me to clasp the patient tightly as she lay on her back, took hold of her leg by the heel, gave it a mighty wrench, and hey presto, the bone was back in its socket and the patient, after a week in bed, little the worse for her accident.

He tackled another case by just as masterly inaction. One day a ganger named Bill ran in, clasping his neck, his boots full of blood and his face drained of colour. His mates explained that a stone had flown up and pierced his neck and that he'd bled 'somethink awful'. I rang the doctor who told me to hold the spot with finger and thumb until he arrived. But the moment Bill let his hand drop from his neck the blood spurted so strongly that we knew the splinter must have pierced the carotid artery. The patient fainted and while Sister ran for restoratives I turned my finger and thumb into a pair of Spencer Wells forceps to close the wound.

Before long Bill came round and grinned, the colour returning to his cheeks and his heart beating normally. He then went to sleep and there we were, this great heavy man literally held between the finger and thumb of a spineless creature with aching arms, tingling fingers and swimming head.

The doctor came at last and lifted my hand. We both watched for the blood to spurt. It didn't. Bill coughed.

'God Almighty!' the doctor exclaimed, 'I wouldn't have believed it, having seen the blood you spilt back there on the line. Go and take a swig of my brandy, matron. Sister, bring the dressings.'

About this time I received the following letter from Lawrence:

Chapala
Jalisco
Mexico
2 July 1923

Dear Miss Skinner,

I have often wondered if you were doing that novel.—Your letter came this morning.

We are going up to New York next week, and maybe to England. I expect to find your Ms. in New York. Then I shall read it carefully, and see what publisher it had best be submitted to. If there are a few suggestions to make, you won't mind, will you. I shall write as soon as I can get through.

Perhaps the best address is:
care Thomas Seltzer, 5 West 50th. Street, New York City.
I often think of Darlington—can see it in my mind's eye as plain as I see the Lake of Chapala in front of me here. Perhaps

we shall come back one day.—The path down the hollow under the gum trees, to your mother's cottage: and those big ducks.—Your mother didn't belong to our broken, fragmentary generation; with her oriental rugs in that little wooden bungalow, and her big, easy gesture of life. It was too small for her, really.

My wife sends many greetings

Yours very sincerely
D. H. Lawrence

I had by this time finished my second novel *Black Swans*, but I now wanted only to go on nursing. I felt like one of the visitants of the forest, a blue wren, perky and self-satisfied. My moulting time was over. This hospital was my territory and I lorded over it. Immigrants ate out of my hand, patients and doctor were well pleased.

That was in July. Towards the end of September I was feeling less content with my lot and the arrival of the following letter further unsettled me.

The Miramar
Santa Monica
Cal.
2 Sept. 1923

Dear Miss Skinner,

I have read 'The House of Ellis' carefully: such good stuff in it; but without unity or harmony. I am afraid as it stands you'd never find a publisher. Yet I hate to think of it all wasted. I like the quality of so much of it. But you have no constructive power.—If you like I will take it and re-cast it, and make a book of it. In which case we should have to appear as collaborators, or assume a pseudonym.—If you give me a free hand, I'll see if I can't make a complete book out of it. If you'd rather your work remained untouched, I will show it to another publisher: but I am afraid there isn't much chance. You have a real gift—there is real quality in these scenes. But without form, like the world before Creation.

I am in California—but don't suppose I shall stay long. Write to me care Thomas Seltzer, 5 West 50th. St., New York.

If I get this book done, we'll publish it in the spring.—And if you agree to my re-casting this: then I wish you would take up that former novel of yours, about the girl and the convict—and break off where the three run away—keep the first part, and continue as a love story or romance, where the love of the girl is divided between the Irish convict and the young gentleman—make it a tragedy if you like—but let the theme be the conflict between the two *kinds* of love in the heart of the girl: her love for Peter (was that the young man's name?)—and her love for the Irish ex-convict. See if you can't carry that out. —Because, of course, as you have it, the convict is the more attractive of the two men, but the less amenable.—Only all that adventure in the N.W. is not very convincing. Keep the story near Perth—or Albany, if you can.

If you see Mr. Siebenhaur tell him I have hopes of Max Havelaar for the spring of next year too.

Best wishes to you all at Leithdale.

Yours very sincerely,
D. H. Lawrence

19

Letters from Lawrence

Back at Darlington once more I was faced with the problem of finalising Mother's affairs, namely wrestling with wills, lawyers and sealing-wax. My brother and sisters had swooped in and been granted their portion after sales of property, furniture and effects. Only Mittie remained in Brook Cottage. Estelle and Dollie had gone off with their husbands to spend their legacies. Nazeli, who had divorced her husband, joined forces with Jack and they bought a shop in East Perth complete with a tumbledown stable and a chestnut racing filly named Rhubarb. Jack, dressed in open-necked shirt and breeches, his battered service hat pulled down over the wounded side of his face, trained the filly in the sandy streets while delivering orders. They were thoroughly enjoying themselves, but as Nazeli had no more idea than a kindly goose of running a shop, it couldn't last. Jack passed Rhubarb over to a trainer and went off to the goldfields while Nazeli, without a stiver of her portion left, returned to Mittie and me in Darlington, bringing her little son Jimmie with her, his sisters Eve and Judy having been taken over by their paternal aunts. Nazeli soon became bored with Darlington so I helped buy her another shop, this time near the sea and a good State school.

Now everyone was happy—except Mittie who, having devoted herself completely to Mother and Jack, was sadly bereft and insisted on paying off the mortgages on the two cottages and settling Jack's debts. Mittie and I were very good friends at that time, but she made my heart ache because she had not found happiness. Industrious, pretty and witty, she was never very wise and always seemed to take the left turn instead of the right. When an eligible suitor sought her hand she immediately fell in love with some poor tutor or a scamp. Oh, why hadn't she married Allistair or Charles or Harry who would have taken care of her?

I prised another slice of my portion from Harold, my lawyer cousin, to have our home put in repair. Harold feared we were heading for disaster but he was impressed when I showed him Lawrence's letters and, convinced I could make money if I took the book to London, he promised I could have the fare in another month or two.

I had been back in Darlington about a month and was doing research for a biography of Lord Forrest when the next news came from Lawrence in Mexico. His letters always put me in a pleasant frame of mind, as you can understand when reading them.

> Hotel Garcia
> Guadalajara
> Jal.
> Mexico
> 1st. Nov. 1923

Dear Miss Skinner,

I have been busy over your novel, as I travelled. The only thing was to write it all out again, following your MS. almost exactly, but giving a unity, a rhythm, and a little more psychic development than you had done. I have now come to Book IV. The end will have to be different, a good deal different.

Of course I don't know how you feel about this. I hope to hear from you soon. But I think, now, the novel will be a good one. I have a very high regard for it myself.—The title, I thought, might be The Boy in the Bush. There have been so many Houses in print.

If possible, I should like to hear from you in time to arrange for publication in England and in America simultaneously in early April. As soon as ever I can, I will have a type-script copy sent to you, with your own MS. Your hero Jack is not quite so absolutely blameless an angel, according to me. You left the character psychologically at a standstill all the way: same boy at the beginning and the end. I have tried, taking your inner cue, to make a rather daring development, psychologically. You may disapprove.

But I think it makes a very very interesting book. If you like, we will appear as collaborators—let the book come out in our joint names. Or we can have a single nom de plume.—And we can go halves in English and American royalties.—All, of course, if you approve.—Then of course I've got the publishers to consider. They will insist on their point of view.

I wanted my wife to come and spend the winter in Mexico.

But she has gone to London and won't come back. She says England is best. So I shall have to go there. Write to me care Curtis Brown, 6 Henrietta St. Covent Garden. W.C.2.
My best wishes to you. I will order you a copy of 'Kangaroo'.

> Yours sincerely,
> D. H. Lawrence
> Hotel Garcia
> Guadalajara
>
> Jal.
> Mexico
> 15th Novem. 1923

Dear Miss Skinner,

I finished the novel yesterday. I call it *The Boy in the Bush.* I think quite a lot of it. Today I am sending the ms. to my agent, Curtis Brown, 6 Henrietta St Covent Garden London W.C.2. His cable address is Browncurt, London.

Curtis Brown will have the MS typed, & the moment I get to London—I hope to be there by Christmas—I will go through it and have a copy sent to you.

Seltzer wants to do the book in New York in April: so that would mean Martin Secker bringing it out at the same time in London. Seltzer suggests my name & yours as joint authors.
I shall wait to hear from you.

> Yours sincerely,
> D. H. Lawrence

It was two months before I heard from him again.

> Care Curtis Brown
> 6 Henrietta St
> Covent Garden
> London W.C.2
> 13th Jan. 1924

Dear Miss Skinner,

I am back as you see in London. Two of your letters have followed me here—also Lord Strathsprey's fume against 'Kangaroo'. Amusing. The reviews were very good here, especially in the Times.

I have got the complete typescript of 'The Boy in the Bush'

now, and am going through it. It's awfully good, I like it immensely. I hope in about four days' time to post you the third of the typed copies. Will go you through it at once, and let me have *by return* any suggestions you can make. Be quick, and you'll be in time for the proofs, I hope. Seltzer wants to do the book in New York in April.

But friends of mine here—John Middleton Murry, & others,—want to set up as publishers, and would like to kick off with 'The Boy in the Bush'. They might be ready for May. But I like to have the publication simultaneous in New York & London. If I don't keep 'The Boy' for Murry, I shall let Secker have it, as he does my other books.—Curtis Brown, whose address I give, will draw up an agreement & send a copy to you to be signed. My idea is to publish under both our names and go halves in the royalties. The preliminary expenses—such as this typing—are mine. Of course publishers are glad to get the MS—they pay us, not we them. But I don't think I'll ask for advance on royalties, unless you wish it. If you *do* wish it, write to Curtis Brown, and say you would like an advance of £25. or £30. Otherwise we get an account at the end of six months, & the money three months later.

I don't care for England—so dark, so wet, so dismal. I think we shall go to Paris next week, and in March back to America. You might, if you have time, send me a letter C/O Curtis Brown & another C/O Seltzer, 5 W. 50th St. New York, simultaneously.

I think very often of you & Miss Beakbane—I'd forgotten her *name*, but not her face—and of your brother out there in W. Australia. I am sure I shall see you again. Hope Letty* goes well. Always write *what you want* to write. Did you mean a biography, or a novel, of the noble Lord.

My wife will write to you.

Yours
D. H. Lawrence

A fortnight later came a postcard from Paris. The picture was of a gargoyle surmounted by a bird on the façade of Notre Dame de Paris—and what did I care if he thought me the gargoyle and himself the bird?

---

* Heroine in *Black Swans.*

Paris
31 Jan.

I have your letter via Curtis Brown, & am returning it to him,
so that he can make the agreement. His cable address is *Browncurt London*. Seltzers is *Letters New York*. Best do everything
through Curtis Brown. I don't know how long I shall stay in
Europe—Perhaps till end of March.

Hope the MS. doesn't alarm you—don't let it, anyhow.

D.H.L.

During this time I had had my teeth out and was fitted with plates.
Oh, ye gods and little fishes, the agony of false teeth in those days!
Mittie fed me on bread and milk and was very good but it was
obvious she was all keyed up for an explosion. Since reading
Lawrence's *The Trespasser*, that merciless exposé of the love affair of
a girl and a married man, she had been frightened to death of the
intentions of the fiendish author towards myself. But worse was in
store when the typescript of *The Boy in the Bush* arrived from New
York. As my eyes were paining in sympathy with my gums I had
put it aside unopened. So Mittie set to and read it herself. Hence
the bottled up rage.

Did it burst! 'How dare you send those stories about Jack to that
odious little redheaded devil who crucifies every soul he meets!
You've got to stop him putting your name on that book. Let him have
it if there's no other way out, but refuse his filthy lucre!'

I was utterly crushed for she was better educated than I, having
finished her schooling in Europe and read as well in French as in
English.

When at last I brought myself to read the script, I found that
Lawrence had twisted its tail, even adding a new character. I saw why
Mittie had fumed, though I myself gloried in the touches Lawrence
had given it. I was dismayed, however, that he had altered the construction and pulled it out of focus towards the end. Jack, the hero
I had drawn, would never have ridden a snorting stallion amongst
the old shellbacks, intent on seducing their daughters.*

---

* According to the Hon. Dorothy Brett in her *Lawrence and Brett*—addressed
to Lawrence—it was actually Frieda Lawrence who suggested the ending for
The Boy in the Bush:

  "What do you think of *The Boy in the Bush*?" you ask me suddenly,
  as we sit resting and drinking tea in the house . . .
  "I like it," I reply, "but I don't like the end. He should have died. A

At last I came to the conclusion that Lawrence would alter the book if I asked him to. So I wrote, thanking him for making such a fine job of it generally, but begging him to twist the tail back into place.

Mittie calmed down when I told her I had written and to further propitiate her I suggested she help me with my biography of Lord Forrest, but it was soon obvious that she was not really interested and in fact resented my writing activities. She would bring me huge untidy bunches of flowers to arrange, send me out to water the garden, to burn the rubbish, drown the kittens, feed the cat, peel the potatoes—any excuse it seemed to get me away from my own work. At other times she would heap coals of fire on my head by bringing dainty afternoon teas for my visitors and keeping the little sitting-room as bright as me laidy's drawing-room.

The tension became unbearable. I tried to reason with her but it was no use and I felt desperately lonely.

At last I went down on my knees and argued with Heaven about being alone, without husband and children to lean on in the griefs, joys, excitements, frustrations, disappointments and adventures of life. I complained of my lot in being forced to fight, to kick against stones, to be betrayed and to love and be loved by the wrong people. One must have someone, I said, to prevent one falling into apathy. One might be an apathetic angel but that would be very dull and if one chose to be a devil one would have no peace.

I had to argue this way for proper religion had long since left me. In India, watching the poor little priests of St Francis of Assisi

---

man like that could never have gone on living; he could never have settled down to an ordered life: the only way out for him was to die."

"I know," you say, "I know. That is how I wrote it first; I made him die—only Frieda made me change it."

Frieda looks up from her embroidery. "Yes," she booms, "I made him change it. I couldn't stand the superiority of the man, always the same self-importance. 'Let him become ordinary,' I said. Always this superiority and death."

"Well," I say, "It's spoiled the book."

"Yes," you say, sighing, "he should have died."

Frieda's eyes begin to dart about. "The Brett always agrees with you; always sticks up for you," she says, challengingly. Neither of us answer. We sip our tea and wonder whether a storm will come up before we fetch the milk."

From Edward Nehls, *D. H. Lawrence, A Composite Biography*, Vol. II, University of Wisconsin Press, 1958, p. 355.

I had yearned to be like them, hugging poverty and humility and back in Australia I had inclined to Catholicism. When nursing at the Quarantine Station, however, where soldiers were dying like flies without priest or clergyman I had to rely—for myself and them—on the familiar Hand and Voice which I was now taking to task for the hardness of my lot. But I never had the last word in those arguments. I was simply told: *You, a nurse, have learnt that a surgeon must hurt to mend.* So I gave up protesting and everything began falling into place beyond my reasoning.

Lawrence had not received my letter, addressed to him in Mexico, when he wrote the following:

> Garland's Hotel
> Suffolk Street
> Pall Mall, S.W.I
> 3rd March 1924

Dear Miss Skinner

The Boy in the Bush is in the printer's hands, both here and in New York. After all Martin Secker is publishing it here: and I am signing a contract for it, drawn up by Curtis Brown. The contract is made between me and the publisher, and I sign on your behalf: and Curtis Brown has an order to pay you one-half of all receipts in England and America, after, of course, his 10% agent's fee has been deducted. It is possible Martin Secker will pay about £100 in advance of royalties—in which case Curtis Brown will at once send you a cheque for £50 or thereabouts. I will have all statement of sales made to you as well as to me. Statements are made on 1st. Oct. and 1st May, each year. Curtis Brown is very strict in business, so you will be quite safe. Write to him and ask anything you want to know. My wife and I are sailing in two days time on the *Aquitania* to New York. Address me there, always, c/o Curtis Brown, 116 West 39th St. New York City. You see the agency operates in both cities.

I am very anxious the book should be a success, & that you should get some money as well as fame. Also I hope you are pleased with it. You may quarrel a bit with the last two chapters. But after all, if a man really has cared and cares, for two women, why should he suddenly shelve either of them? It seems to me more immoral suddenly to drop all connection with one of them, than to wish to have the two.

Write to me to New York. I expect we shall go to New

Mexico, and then down to Old Mexico. But letters will come on.

The book, unfortunately, has been delayed here, and Secker will probably not have it out till early June. Seltzer in America will probably be sooner—May, or even end of April. We shall see. You can write to Curtis Brown both in London & New York (in N.Y. the manager is Mr Barmby) for all information. I will see you get six presentation copies from Secker, & six from Seltzer.

I hope now I have thought of everything.

I am not sorry to go back to America: Europe seems to me weary and wearying.
Best wishes to you. My wife sends her regards and remembrances. One day we shall meet again, & laugh things over, I know.

Yours sincerely,
D. H. Lawrence

Soon I will write you a really long letter! Meanwhile all good luck to the boy! Yours very sincerely

Frieda Lawrence

This was followed soon afterwards by a letter from Mexico:

Taos
New Mexico
U.S.A.
4 April 1924

Dear Miss Skinner

Your letter about the *Boy* MS. has come here. I have written to Secker & Seltzer to make the alterations you wish, if it is not too late. Also I tell them they may leave out both chapters at the end, if they wish. But here, if the book is set up, the publishers will not agree unless they wish to of their own account. We shall see. I asked them both to write you what they are doing. The book should be out end of May. It is between-seasons, but I think perhaps it is just as well. Book trade alas is very bad. I have arranged with Curtis Brown's representative in New York to conduct all my business this side. He is

> A. W. Barmby,
> Curtis Brown Ltd.
> 116 West Thirty-ninth St
> New York.

Write to him for anything you want to know. And I will see he sends you your half of the royalties, & the statements, as they come due.

I think myself *The Boy* is a fine book. It runs on to its inevitable conclusions. But I know the world doesn't like the inevitable.—Anyhow I am glad you like it on the whole. I wanted you to say just what you felt—and I do understand your feeling about the things you would like modified. It is a pity we were so far apart, that we could not have worked a bit together.—Now, the next phase is in the hands of the public.

I had a letter also today from Mrs. Throssell. I hope you will get to know her.

We are here again at the foot of the Rockies on the desert, among the Indians—7,000 feet up. I am glad to be away again. The winter in Europe wearied me inexpressibly. There seems a dead hand over the old world.

Tell me what you are doing about a new book.

Many greetings from my wife and me

D. H. Lawrence

That settled it. It was out of my hands. All I had to do was to keep steady and be grateful for such kindness from the stranger who had crossed my path. The book seemed to be delayed, so I hoped he would be able to alter it after all. Anyway I decided I should go to London at once and try to place 'Black Swans' before taking over Leithdale again as I had agreed to do.

Cash, or rather the want of it, was the difficulty. My cousin Harold shook his head. 'Better go to the races on Saturday and put a fiver on Rhubarb,' he said. So Mittie and I went to the races and backed the filly for a place. She ran third, her fetlock having broken near the post, letting two others past her, and had at once to be shot.

With my winnings, I took a return steerage passage to London on the mail steamer leaving in a few days. Mittie went to stay with friends in the country and we let the cottage for ten shillings per week to an old couple who agreed to take care of the property.

Now all there was to do before leaving was to see Nazeli. Heaven above! The shop—with my name on it—had got into much the same state as the other in East Perth and Jimmie, now aged nine, was merrily running it. 'Whoop!' he said. 'Now don't start interfering, Aunt Mollie, I can manage.' His dear little face was filthy, his eyes sparkling. 'Mum's in bed with the doctor. She's got Spanish flu she took from the dead butcher when she was helping Mrs Elks to nurse him. Mum helped lay him out and then went to the funeral with Mrs Elks before she took bad.'

Nazeli certainly had the flu. What was I to do? I called on Heaven, and Jenny Wren, who had been a housemaid at Leithdale, came bounding along the street. She had heard of Nazeli's predicament and being out of a job had come along to give her a hand. Thank God for the Jenny Wrens of this poor world of ours! She took over and didn't she laugh when she saw me off on the boat and found I was travelling steerage. 'You'll do me!' she chuckled, 'and I won't let on to Miss Beakbane, I promise you.' She fluttered round, making what used to be called 'glad eyes' at the sailors, and brought me a letter she found on the first class letter rack. Sent down by the lawyer, it contained an American cheque for one hundred dollars from the mysterious Seltzer's firm in New York.

20

A Life in My Hands

Out to sea from Fremantle next morning I wondered how I would be able to endure the voyage. My shared cabin, below decks and over the engines, was stifling; the meals were unspeakable; the passengers rude and uncouth—they didn't like the look of me, and I didn't like the look of them.

Then came a bellboy yelling round the crowded poop: 'If there's a nurse here, report to the purser, please!'

There was no other nurse. I had no uniform or credentials but I went to the purser's office. I was conducted by an immaculate steward called Albert to a first class single cabin with a porthole, cupboards, washbasin and elaborate fittings.

There I caught sight of my face in the mirror—young looking for my age, I thought, but my wavy hair, usually covered with a veil, was now snow-white. I was ghastly pale from the effects of a night in the nether world. There were smudges round my eyes and my scarred lip seemed more than ever obvious. My eyes, still unusually blue, looked back at me in such astonishment that I laughed.

'What's all this?' I asked the steward.

Albert allowed a smile to light his solemn face. 'A pity we had to haul a nurse from the steerage,' he said, 'but the stewardesses has their hands full like the rest of us. I got a lot of cabins to see to as well as wait on Captain's table, then Mr Cripps has to take crook. He's a cranky cove, but the women are all mad about him. Keeps hisself to hisself, though. He's a bachelor and they say he's one of the world's best engineers. They reckon his appendix is bust and there's no hope for him, but the Sydney surgeon aboard and the ship's doc has him on the table under the knife. All you got to do is stand by while he goes west as the saying is. I'll send a boy along with your tea and don't ring unless you has to.' He was gone.

134

So this was where the Hand had pushed me, just as I had set out to seek fame and fortune as a novelist. I grimaced at the mirror, turned, rolled back the bedclothes on the bunk, and made a list of things required to give a boy to take to the dispensary. They were brought, and then the patient, deeply under chloroform, was carried in, followed by the ship's doctor, harassed and irritable. He said there was a large tube in the incision and he supposed I knew how to keep it in place. 'Not that it matters,' he added, 'for we don't think the patient'll last the night.' He went on his way, telling me not to send for him as there was nothing more to be done.

This sounds callous, but nurses know that a doctor is never so callous as he sounds, and that when he has finished his particular job he leaves it to the nurse to carry on. So there I was left with a stranger named Mr Cripps, and he with me.

I was determined that he should not die, that his guardian angel—and mine—would fight the dark demon that stood at his side. I saw that he was warm and comfortable, but his breathing was shallow, his pulse soft, his handsome clean-shaven face dewy and dank.

There was nothing more to do just then and I grew hungry as scents of succulent fare wafted from the dining-room, the dinner gong sounded and I heard the first class passengers going in to dine.

Ages later Albert slipped in with more hot water, closed the port, snapped on the light over the patient's head and hurried wordlessly away.

Waves began to sweep over the porthole glass, winds whistled, the ship lurched giddily, and doors slammed as passengers raced to their cabins.

I felt I had been swallowed by a whale and was gasping in its belly while its eye turned in to watch me die. I vomited into the basin, wishing I could.

Then the patient opened vacant eyes and began his chloroform vomiting, much accentuated, and I had to forget myself in care for him. It was essential to hold the tube in position by pressing the incision together with both hands, to keep the kidney dish under his chin amidst the towels, to moisten his lips with water and wipe his brow. This I did, periodically leaning sideways over the basin in agony.

Hour after hour went by and no one came near, though once, casting my eyes up to the mirror, I saw the shadowy form of the nightwatchman come to the door and go.

When the storm passed and dawn sent a shaft of light over the waters, I felt better; and the patient had not died. Indeed, he became like a fractious boy. 'I want a drink of water. I must have a long drink of water. If you won't let me have a drink of water, turn me on my side and let me die.'

Telling him for the fiftieth time he couldn't have a long drink and that I couldn't turn him over without help, I lost my temper. That astonished him to silence. He lifted his square chin grimly, and shut his eyes. Then I loved him with great tenderness and great pride and, knowing that he would live, turned away and sat on the plush seat under the porthole, waiting for Albert.

When he came in with morning tea he stepped gingerly, eyebrows raised.

'The patient is O.K., Albert, but I'm not so good. Stay a few minutes please and help me turn him on his side. Then report to the doctor and say I'm not staying here another minute. I can't take any more.'

But relief did not come—nor breakfast—for many hours. With sagging knees and burning eyes I sat like a Hindu image on the plush seat, rising to tend my patient when necessary, until at last he asked me where the devil I came from and who I was.'

'A steerage passenger,' I said, 'and back there I'll go as soon as the doctor sends relief.'

'Oh no you won't,' he answered. And then I told him I was sorry to have spoken so crossly to him when he came to.

'If you had messed me up with kisses and tears I should have died,' he grinned, 'but when you spoke as no one before since I was a kid, I knew I wouldn't die. You held me back all night with your hands and I hated you: and now I'm not going to part with you. You see I'm scared. I've been in some awful places but was never scared before. Please stay with me.'

'That's impossible,' I grinned back.

The long and short of it was that he made it possible for me to have a cabin-de-luxe for five hours sleep a day and a deck chair in the annexe at night. He refused to be taken off at Colombo by his engineering company and we became firm friends. He saw no visitors —except once, the Bishop of Hong Kong—not even Mr (later Sir) Earle Page, M.P., and certainly not the Merry Widow of that ship.

The only bone of contention between us—a bitter one to me—

was that I was collaborating with D. H. Lawrence. If it had been Lawrence of Arabia it would have been a different matter. He was that sort of man.

He handed me an envelope when we landed. 'A token of appreciation,' he said. It contained a requital of my return fare. He invited me to visit his mother and took me out to lunch on our arrival in London. But I knew our interests were far apart, and said adieu without regrets.

21

The Boy in the Bush

It was a cocky heedless sparrow that came to London in the early summer of 1924, though not quite so cocky when she walked out of the office of Curtis Brown. His lady secretary saw to that. She said Mr Lawrence was not in London but she would send on any correspondence if I left my address. No, she told me, it was no use my going to see Mr Secker, he was on holiday, and so was Mr Curtis. If I considered the manuscript I had with me so promising, why not take it to Cape's publishing house in Henrietta Street myself? This bit of advice I never unravelled but took it, not aware that Cape's was at the time considered the most exclusive publishing firm in London.

Mr Cape must have been somewhat startled at the appearance of a sparrow in his office, but he handed me on to his reader Mr Edward Garnett, who was a friend of D. H. Lawrence. Mr Garnett, looking like a white bulldog, merely said, 'Leave your address and the script on my desk and I'll have a look at it. Go and have a fly round and don't worry us again unless we send for you.'

It's hard to explain how happy I was then, and how quite convinced I was that God's Hand was on my shoulder, using me for His Own Purpose. Awful cheek when one comes to think of it—and I mean awful. But that's the simple truth, and it carried me along most happily.

I stayed with my ageing Aunt Minnie, who now took no notice of my generation, which left me free to hop, skip and jump, and while doing so I heard from Lawrence again.

Del Monte Ranch
Questa
New Mexico
8 July 1924

Dear Miss Skinner,

I was very much surprised to get your ship-board letter, & to know that by now you will be in London. I hope you will have a good time: & that you won't be disappointed at waiting until September 1st for *The Boy*. Secker sent me his advertisement leaflet: too bad that he leaves you out so much: it is not *my* wish, not a bit: just a publisher's attempt to use a known name & suppress an unknown one. I hope *Lettie* meets with a warm reception. What do you say you'll call it? *Black Swans* sounds nice, to me.

I am sorry we shan't be seeing you. We are here on this ranch, which now belongs to my wife—it is fine and wild. But I want to go down to Old Mexico in the autumn, to finish a novel I began there.

I have written you several letters since we have been back in America: they take so long. Also Seltzer is supposed to have sent you a hundred dollars advance on royalties, for *The Boy*. As soon as I had your letter, I wrote and asked him, if he had not sent the cheque to Australia, to send it to you in London. Anyhow I hope it will turn up.—If you need a few pounds, tell Curtis Brown, and they can always get you £25 or £30 advance from Martin Secker.

Be sure and let me know how you find London, and how Lettie is received. I shall be very much interested to read her again.
I think *The Boy* will be translated at once into German.
All good wishes to you from my wife and me

Yours sincerely
D. H. Lawrence

Tell Curtis Brown I wanted a few pounds? Not if I was starving. I never saw him, never went to the office again. This was a bit of pride that proved unfortunate for me later, but you know how it is— some have one sort of pride, some another. I didn't even go back to demand that my signature be added to the contract for *The Boy in the Bush*, though the secretary sent business letters on to me through the Agent General's office, enclosing half royalties now and again. As for Secker and Seltzer, they remained as complete strangers to me as peregrine falcons.

Since I trusted Lawrence (who never failed me) and he trusted Curtis Brown, that was enough for me. So buoyant and happy as life unfolded itself, I fluttered around.

First it was in green pastures staying with Nellie Beakbane's Quaker folk in the near country. How lovely to walk down old English villages, to smell the old English flowers and hay, and in the lanes the sharp odour of mint, shepherd's purse and dog-roses; to walk in fields under oak and elm or in parklands around the ancient houses, aloof, isolated, but English in their every detail.

The village of Jordons in particular gave peace to my restless heart. Here at the Quaker meeting house an Oxford don lectured on science, ending with a reference to Mallory lost on Everest. 'When the Spirit of Endeavour dies, all that is best in mankind will be lost.'

A visit to Worcester gave me something too. I was spending the day with Sir Robert Scallon whom I had nursed in India. All his gallant life was behind him, but behind that was tradition. He had done his duty according to his principles and was content. He took me down to the old green silent river to see the wall marked by its risings over many generations, and into the cathedral to visit the tomb of one of my Skinner ancestors—perhaps the bishop who was beheaded for his principles in the reign of Bloody Mary.

When I returned to London in August, I had found again 'the spirit of endeavour' and the resolve to hold to my own principles even should I lose my head for it. Perhaps Lawrence had sown the seeds. Perhaps too because I had begun to find in the Quaker philosophy the spiritual guidance I had lost with Sybil's death.

Back in London, my relations, rather chary of me, stood back till an invitation came, sent from the Agent General's office, to a garden party at Buckingham Palace. Then they rallied, saw to it that my clothes were right and found the son of Sir Redvers Buller (a friend of my father's) and his wife who were glad to accompany the Australian cousin.

The Bullers proved ideal for this role. They looked top-hole and knew everyone of note—by sight at any rate.

Guests entered by the back gate of the palace garden and then everything was like the world of Alice Through the Looking Glass. King George V, a little man in grey, strolled the lawns with his tall black-garbed equerries. No one wore uniform except some Indian officers who made a splash of colour in their turbans and exotic outfits of red and blue. There, in a group apart with their sister the Princess Royal were the Prince of Wales and Dukes of York, Gloucester and Kent. Of them all only Albert of York was as yet married and the Bullers, with chuckles of delight, showed me his wife Elizabeth, so full of life and happiness and the darling of everyone's heart. Gossip had it that she was defiant to Queen Mary, daring to shorten her frocks when told to lengthen them.

Queen Mary, in a very long pale blue gown, appeared last of all and was accompanied by the Queens of Spain and Italy, each with teen-age daughters. We stood near Margot Asquith as she kept an admiring circle of actors and actresses in fits of suppressed laughter. 'There goes the new Labour Premier,' we heard her say, 'this time *not* in his fireman's uniform. He attended the levee in it, you know, and the King said to him, "Do you have to carry that heavy helmet? I don't have to carry my crown about." '

While taking refreshments in a large marquee, I saw Queen Mary in her own tent wolfing strawberries and cream as if she had never tasted them before.

The Bullers had met up with friends so I made my excuses and slipped away up the terraces and into the palace to inspect the drawing-rooms with which I was familiar from the paintings of Winterhalter, finding them just as he had painted them in Queen Victoria's time. I enquired meekly of the tall footman in red with white stockings and buckled shoes if I might make my exit by the front door. He bowed and so down the sweep of front steps of Buckingham Palace hopped the sparrow and along the drive it flew and out of the iron gates.

And then it was the end of August and I received this letter from Lawrence.

Del Monte Ranch
Questa
New Mexico
10 Aug 1924

Dear Miss Skinner,
I had a copy of *The Boy* from Secker: looks very nice. Seltzer will distribute for you six complimentary copies in America— or anywhere—if you send him addresses. We did the American jacket between us—rather nice.—
I want to hear more of your London experiences, & how "Letty" is looking.—

Seltzer wrote that he sent you some time ago a cheque for $100⁰⁰ to Australia. Hope you get it safely.—And I hope you'll shortly get £10 from Curtis Brown for German translation of *The Boy*. It's already being done.

Let me know how you have fared, & if you had a good time.

Yrs

D. H. Lawrence

At the beginning of September *The Times* and *Morning Post* both printed long reviews of *The Boy in the Bush* and Mr. Siebenhaur (who had met Lawrence at Leithdale) invited me to accompany him to Fleet Street day by day to examine the files for further comments. We found dozens of them, and split our sides with laughter as we read them over cups of tea in little coffee inns frequented by scurrying journalists.

What amused us so much was that M. L. Skinner was a riddle—a thorn in the critics' flesh. Even Mr Curtis Brown or Mr Seltzer apparently could not or would not give them the identity of D. H. Lawrence's collaborator. *The Weekly Westminster* capped it in two columns with: 'My theory of M. L. Skinner is that "there is no such person".' The *Bookshelf* said something about Lawrence cutting in on Skinner's kangaroo hunt with a description of coo-eeing, 'then Lawrence steps back and off goes Skinner again after his roo.'

The *Sketch* (Keble Howard) was pleasing. 'I do not know who M. L. Skinner may be . . . It may be a gentleman or it may be lady,' but 'Len is a great creation in fiction . . . I am sure he is drawn by the pen—or the pens—of a master.'

Edwin Muir of *The Nation*, though ignoring Skinner, finished up with: 'The present volume shows a general speeding up. If we have to thank Mr Lawrence's collaborator for this we can only pray that the collaboration will continue.'

I felt as proud as a saltbush chat finding herself cooed at in a dovecote.

It may seem odd that I wasn't terribly interested in the actual copies I received from Secker at the end of the month. I don't even know what became of them. That it was reviewed by the best papers enthralled me.

The following note came to hand during this time and naturally I felt proud and warm in my thoughts for this brilliant and famous author who was so kind and generous to me.

Del Monte Ranch
Questa
New Mexico
13 Sept. 1924

Dear Molly Skinner

Your letter from Stourport today—I saw *The Times* review: it's too bad they leave you out: and it's not my fault, I assure you. I do hope *Black Swans* is going well. Get the opinion of somebody competent. Write to Mrs. Catherine Carswell 110 heath St. Hampstead N.W.3. She is our very good friend, & wrote two good novels. She is in the country—but write to her and meet her. She can help you probably. She understands publishers and so on.—Do you take notice what cowardly reviewers say about me—quelle canaille! If I'd listened to reviewers I shouldn't exist.—We are all well—leave for Mexico proper in October.—Didn't you get a good cheque from Curtis Brown? Secker said he paid one in. I think if you press Curtis Brown, he will get you an *advance* from Secker. Do it. And I hope you have Seltzer's $100^{00}.

Best wishes to you from us both

D.H.L.

Meanwhile reviews went on livening my days. I wouldn't have missed them for anything. Was this one of Heaven's little jokes? I didn't try to understand it. For a time the reviews called me 'Mr Skinner', and shoved me aside with some contempt. The *British Australian* praised *The Boy*; *John o'London* jeered at him; *The Daily Telegraph* did both; *The Daily Mail* affirmed that 'all their characters are alive' and *Truth* that it was 'a vigorous and gripping story . . . as much psychological as episodical'; *The Daily Graphic, Ladies Pictorial, Saturday Review, Spectator, Westminster Gazette, Current Thought, New Statesman, Country Life, Evening News* all had their say before Mr Skinner was discovered to be a Miss.

But how many writers appeared to hate Lawrence! Joseph Clayton, who had placed *Letters of a V.A.D.* and liked it very much, proved no exception but he and his wife took me to a cocktail party given by the Chestertons in the flat they gloried in. We got there via an alley off the Strand, stumbling over dust-bins, and up a winding stair to find Chesterton's sister-in-law in a kitchen done out in black and white like a stage set. She handed us on to the great Chesterton, who conveyed us to a room packed with literary notables, announcing with his famous chuckle, 'The Claytons and Miss Skinner, Lawrence's collaborator in *The Boy in the Bush*.'

Everything grew muddled in a din of hilarity. No name reached me, I only know they were the literati of the day. A fair girl sat at my feet, and a charming young man took charge of me. At last I met someone who loved Lawrence and who took me on the roof where the younger set were sporting with Japanese lanterns. It was the evening after the Eton and Harrow match and shouts of joy echoing from the Strand, mingling with their laughter, made the atmosphere more than ever festive.

When we went for our wraps we found that some of these remarkable people had turned the double bed into a stage and were acting a play which one of them had just written. They were so pleased with their fun that they hired a theatre and put it on the boards the following week. It ran two nights.

22

London and the Arts

Though he gave no indication of it to me, Lawrence was undoubtedly then at the beginning of his fierce battle against the disease that was to consume his life.

Others have cast merciless light on his moods, his perversity, cantankerousness and arrogance but what I have to tell of him is of the tenderness, kindness and understanding he showed to a simple sparrow. He had, as Aldous Huxley wrote to me later, an 'almost superhuman quality of vision' and I felt that he saw me now, confident, don't-careish and grinning like a Cheshire cat as I prowled round London.

There was a great change in this city's social atmosphere since the war. Women had gained the vote ten years before and seemed more masculine, free and bold. Even spinsters were jolly, but there were too many of them. Three to one didn't seem fair, but it did much to change the double standard of former generations. To my utter astonishment I found that one of my spinster cousins had a little boy of six. In this case, the father of the boy, a young officer, still wanted to marry her—and eventually did. But there were others who never married and were proud of their motherhood.

I was staying now with my naughty elderly cousin Lil who in my youth was cold-shouldered by the strait-laced Skinners. It was she who now cold-shouldered them, but she took the colonial cousin around and gave her a hectic time amongst her artist, writer and musician friends. Chuckling over the fact that dear Jim's innocent daughter had collaborated with the notorious Lawrence, she read with glee the critiques that continued to pour in from all over England, Scotland, Ireland and soon from Germany.

I sparkled in her company and listened wide-eyed when she held forth in this vein: 'Visionary habits must be acquired to understand

145

what Lawrence means, though so far he has no rigorous classicism even regarding sex. He *would* marry the woman he loved though she is of a different social class and had to leave her husband and children for him.' Or, 'Only visionary imagination can find the material to paint a picture or write a worth-while book.' Or, 'Action is only the primitive force of spontaneous energy, and energy when thwarted can endanger the artist's spiritual power.'

A number of people I met talked a fashionable jargon largely based on Freudian psychology—but I appreciated an ugly girl called Jane who one day remarked, 'I learnt when mixing paints that the spiritual universe permeates the material. The weakness of human nature is diffused with redeeming grace.'

I liked this girl and went to see her in her studio, pretending to know what she was talking about as she showed the canvases stacked in her windowed attic. 'These are realistic, these impressionistic— contradictions of course but they lead to surrealism and then more abstract forms—expressionism, cubism and so forth. They all help me find my medium which is interior decoration.' She pulled a face. 'One must not let the public see that one's theme is the cry of the human heart, or one would not earn a living.'

'You certainly hide it well,' I said, looking at her startling abstract shapes. I could have bitten my tongue out, but she only laughed and replied, 'So do you, if your *Boy in the Bush* is a reflection of yourself.'

'Not in the last two chapters!' I said. 'Those are Lawrence.'

'Not Lawrence but his craft,' she said. 'He has learned,' she grimaced, 'how to intrigue his public. That's all.'

One day Cousin Lil said, 'I looked in at Jane's studio this morning to give her a note about a commission but she roared like a bull at me so I got out. I forgot to leave the message so perhaps you'd take it round to her.'

The ugly girl, whose door was unlocked, was lying on a couch staring at the fanlight. I thought she must be either drugged or drunk but, determined she should have the note, I went over and put it in her hand. She swung round to a sitting position, pulled me down beside her, then put her untidy head on my shoulder and wept.

The nurse instinct rose in me at once. Without speaking I put my arm round her and presently she was unburdening her passionate heart.

'I gave Gloria everything I had,' she said. 'She was down and out

. . . gin and drugs. She is lovely—a model—but she'd been discarded
. . . a baby you know . . . a flashy little thing, we called it Fay and
handed it over to an orphanage where we could see it sometimes. I
took Gloria in, loved her and cared for her. You wouldn't understand
a woman's love for a woman.'

'Wouldn't I?'

'If you do, what would you do about it?'

'Run away. Go on.'

'It's she who ran. I thought she loved me . . . in fact I was sure
of it. Oh gosh, she was so entrancing to me . . . gay even when she
was thin and suffering. She declared I gave her back her strength and
will to live. She gave up the grog and the drugs and started model-
ling again. But she told me she depended on me for her very life
and she loved me better than anyone in the world except Fay whom
we both adored. I believed her—and now I can't bear it!' she
stormed, rising and walking like a caged tiger up and down the
studio. 'Read this!' she thrust me a note written on pink scented
paper and I read a message to this effect:

> Dear Jane,
> I've gone to France with André. Thanks for all you've done but
> I can't stand being your friend any longer and Fay is a burden.
> I must have fun and live my own life.
>
> Cheerio.
> Gloria

The girl's grief and anguish stunned me and I found myself
repeating to her what she had said about the weakness of human
nature and the spiritual being stronger than the material. Then I
quoted that cry of another mortal's agony from the 55th psalm.

> For it is not an open enemy, that hath done me this dishonour:
> for then I could have borne it. Neither was it mine adversary,
> that did magnify himself against me: for then peradventure I
> would have hid myself from him. But it was even thou, my
> companion . . . We took sweet counsel together . . .

And I went on stumblingly to tell her to cast her burden on the
Lord. She raised her hand, I thought to slap my face, then she
grinned, called me a queer fish, lit the primus and made coffee. With
a cup in one hand she turned the easel round and pointed to what
she had been painting just before her friend had left. The composi-

tion held no meaning for me but as she looked at it the heavy lines went out of her face and the sparkle returned to her eyes. 'I shall call it *The Awakening*,' she said. 'It's a mural. Now I'll put some of my suffering into it and I expect it will bring me fame. Thank you for coming, you lunatic!'

One day I was invited by Catherine Carswell to lunch with her in a restaurant. I found her as chary of me in one way as my relations in another but I think she and her husband were the kindest friends Lawrence ever had in the literary world. They had known him for a long time and understood that in spite of his genius, or perhaps because of it, he could not help behaving at times like a fractious high-spirited boy. She said nothing about it now, nor of how he was hounded and booed, reviled, and reluctantly admired when he booed back and went racing on in front of the pack. She did not tell how, when he had been in England not so long before, he had almost persuaded her and her husband to join the dream community he called 'Rananim' in Mexico where all were to work together in the 'real decency which is in each member of the community'. No, she was just a charming everyday hostess who took off her gloves and ate her lunch as if she enjoyed it—a little bit bored perhaps over dropping breadcrumbs for a sparrow. We corresponded later and came to understand each other better through the written word.

By September the lovely golden-brown foliage never seen on Australian trees began to fall and swirl over the dewy vivid green lawns in the parks, and the dank soil had taken all the bulbs and flower seeds back to her bosom until the spring.

Nellie Beakbane, wishing to avoid another winter in England, had already sailed back home and as the fogs gathered around the crowded blocks of flats I too felt an overpowering urgency to return. I booked my passage, giving up the idea I had had of waiting to hear from Jonathan Cape. Then came a letter asking me to call on him.

Mr Cape with his long elegantly trousered legs under a polished table handed me on to Edward Garnett who, carelessly dressed, large, clumsy, kindly and sincere, was nearer my heart.

He began at once to roar and growl and thump the table.

'This book,' he said, 'is so damn, damn bad that it sends me crazy because it is also—Whatever are you crying for?' He took a huge handkerchief from his pocket and wiped my tears away. 'Look here,

I was going to say it's so damn, damn good as well we are going to publish it; and you must go back to Australia and write the best novel that ever came out of it.'

In this prediction Edward Garnett made one of his very rare mistakes. He was London's acknowledged grandest critic. They say he persuaded John Galsworthy to rewrite his first novel over and over again until he found his own style; that he *made* his great friend, Joseph Conrad; was D. H. Lawrence's stay and support; and later launched H. E. Bates on his successful career. He couldn't do much with me, for I was soon too far away from his kindly interest, but he did his best. The blessed man had taken copious notes on my manuscript, pointing out its weaknesses, and these he now presented to me.

He also asked me to tea in his Chelsea diggings—an old house where the blackberries outside the mullioned windows cast shadows on the green table, the uncarpeted floor and the packed bookcases and where, even when the sunshine pierced the blue mist of the river, the shades of writers seemed forever passing in and out.

The table was set with thick cups and saucers, the kettle on the hob, and while Mr Garnett made tea he asked me to mark the parts I had written in his copy of *The Boy in the Bush*.

After tea we talked of Lawrence without any reserve whatever.

'I've watched him,' Mr Garnett said, 'since he came riding into the arena of literature on a hollow-backed mule, flourishing a thorned stick blossoming with odd flowers. With this he hit his opponents and floored 'em. He watered the flowers with pain and grief, pruned them with bleeding fingers, tended them with obstinate care and avoided grafting from other writers. I first sought him out after reading some of his contributions to magazines. I found that he was a schoolmaster, rather frail then, with an ordinary face and keen blue eyes—'

'Not always blue, Mr Garnett,' I interrupted. 'Hazel, green, beryl, as the mood takes him.'

'So his fatal fascination for women got you too.'

I told him that his looks—apart from his eyes—had no appeal for me and that his hands reminded me of those in paintings of Queen Victoria's daughters.

'Still, he does fascinate women,' he said. 'He always has. He shocked my wife and myself profoundly when we asked him to stay with us in our country house and he played havoc with the girls in the village. We didn't know till the vicar complained, admitting to our amazement that his own daughter was the chief victim. When we had it out with Lawrence he only said, "All right, there are plenty of girls in the parks!" and made off, sending a heartless telegram from London to the vicar's daughter. That was shocking— well, you know what a village postmistress is, and soon everyone was sniggering over the tea tables.'

It was clear that Mr Garnett's love of literature was greater than his concern for village scandal, for he introduced the naughty young man to many famous writers as time went on. 'He was so uncouthly rude to them that they shunned him before long—the men I mean. The women seemed to like his rudeness and he made amazing friendships with them.' Garnett shoved his fingers through his hair and looked at me quizzically. 'I'm not saying that the fellow didn't make firm friends with grand men too—he's a peculiar sort of genius, I'm convinced, exciting and perverse and very sure of himself. What confounds me is that he chose *you* to collaborate with. While working on this *Boy in the Bush* he behaved outrageously, even to the gentle Frieda. In fact his furies and tantrums were so bad that she actually left him. Then he came back from Mexico lately and took her off with him. Now tell me what you think of all that?'

I told him that Lawrence's letters to me showed no sign of what he spoke of; nor did his behaviour when in Australia.

'Tut, tut,' Mr Garnett said. 'His tantrums go to such an extent that he sometimes breaks crockery over his good Frieda's head . . .'

'Frieda probably enjoys it,' I told him. 'After all a woman who can leave her husband and children for a man with no earthly security must love him a lot.'

Mr Garnett shook his head. 'I don't understand it, even though I have stood by David from first to last.'

'I do. The power of love between twin souls is beyond sex and shatters all argument.' I stood up, adding with a grin, 'At Leithdale he showed nothing but gentleness and consideration. He sat with me outside the laundry and left a few seeds to sow in the kitchen garden of my mind.'

Mr Garnett jumped up from his chair and held out his hand.

'Well, be off with you and plant the seedlings in that wild and woolly garden of yours. Stay in your own country and cultivate them carefully. I am convinced you will write something better than *Black Swans* before you've done.'

Somewhat perturbed I returned to Aunt Minnie's where I was sure of finding a good dinner and peaceful oblivion from conflicting thoughts. But before long I found something more reassuring than anything else in the following letter.

Hotel Francia
Oaxaca
Mexico
17 Nov 1924

Dear Mollie Skinner

I'm glad Jonathan Cape is going to do *Black Swans*, and even that Edward Garnett roars at you to make you do it better. He was a very good friend of mine, old Edward.

The Boy seems to be doing very well over here, though they say business is bad in the U.S.A. Anyhow Seltzer seems pleased. We are here way down in the south of Mexico, with brilliant sunshine every day, & warm. My wife and I are moving into a house, to stay a few months if we like it, & if I can get on with the novel I have a good deal written. But I get a bit tired of the American Continent after a certain time: it is so hard and jolting, & I want to go away. Sometimes I feel very much like going to West Australia again, & going way down to the south coast, where the sands are white & the big trees stand up to the sea. I feel very much attracted that way. Do you think I should like it?

I shall be so glad to see *Black Swans* sailing out with folded wings. Send it me as soon as it is out, so that I can see what you've done with it, & how you have come on.

Greetings from my wife and me

D. H. Lawrence

23

Death of a Digger

Jauntily I stepped off the ship at Fremantle, thinking of myself as a coming author—and came quickly down to earth.

I returned to Darlington, Leithdale and Nellie Beakbane who, though our friendship was assured, resented my writing, since it took from her some of the attention she had a right to expect.

I planned to write a novel of the goldfields but for this reason did not start at once, although there was time to spare, as our house guests were then few and Mittie, always friendly with my partner, was buzzing around. Mittie had apparently forgotten her antagonism towards *The Boy in the Bush* and approved of my receiving the following letter from Frieda Lawrence, whom she considered charming and aristocratic.

Oaxaca
Mexico
3.1.25

Dear Miss Skinner,

A happy new year to you! I have written you many letters in the spirit only, when one was finished, another was ready, so they were never born in the flesh! I am very glad your Black Swans are going to appear—Don't let the critics worry you, Lawrence *never* reads their criticism only I get mad occasionally—This is to welcome you in Australia, you will have the other half of life again, that you don't get in London—I hope one day you will come and see us at the ranch, I love it—This is a strange country, quite fantastic in its wild politics or no politics, but you will read it in Lawr's next novel. I like it by far the best!! London to me is a wilderness and rabble, but just a few people! You will be on the sea now—we may go to Europe before long!

All good luck to you and the 'swans'. Yours
Frieda Lawrence

A couple of months later came another letter which revived my desire to write the goldfields book which I was to call 'Eve in the Land of Nod'.

Del Monte Ranch
Questa
New Mexico
21 April 1925

Dear Mollie Skinner,

Your letter of 26th Feb. today. We were thinking about you and wondering about *Black Swans*. I'm looking forward to reading it soon. When is it due? I'm sure it's best for it to appear absolutely without any connection with me. That way you'll exist in yourself and by yourself, for the tribe. I'll write an introduction to your third novel, if you like.—It's time we should be getting statements of sales for the Boy.—It's always a long time before the money comes in: but it will come.

I'll send you my new novel *St. Mawr* when I get it: or I'll ask Secker to post it direct. It is due in May.

You know, we got back here two weeks ago. I was awfully ill in Mexico—thought I was never going to get out, malaria, typhoid condition inside, and chest going wrong with flu. Still have a cough and have to stay a good deal in bed. But glad to be back on our own ranch. We have a young Indian couple, Trinidad & his wife Puffina, looking after us. It has been hot and sunny—but today cold & crumbling snow, and I'm in bed.— Don't bother about critics and immediate returns. Writing, essentially, is its own reward. If it's a joy—and a pain—to you, struggling & producing a book—then go ahead, and never mind the rest. Write when there comes a certain passion upon you, and revise in a later, warier, but still sympathetic mood.

I got my novel *Quetzalcoatl* done in Mexico: at a tremendous cost to myself. Feel I don't want ever to see it again. Loathe the thought of having to go over it and prune and correct, in typescript.

I expect we shall be here all summer. We want to go to Europe in September.—You won't be happy in that little cottage on the creek-slope unless you work.—Why not write your *mother's* novel?

Yrs
D. H. Lawrence

And then suddenly Mittie was called to the bedside of Judy, Nazeli's little girl, as the paternal aunt who cared for her had gone North, leaving the child in a private hospital after some illness. Nazeli was out of it for she had fled with young Jimmie to some job far inland, leaving the shop a dismal wreck.

Distracted, Mittie phoned that Judy was in a bad way and asked me to come and share the responsibility. I was planning to join her when a telegram came from Southern Cross to say that Jack was seriously ill with pneumonia. He was pronounced out of danger by the time I arrived but the doctor asked me to stay for a few days at the district hospital to help Sister Munroe.

By this time many government and district hospitals had been leased to nurses to run as best they could without subsidy. It proved an impossible task, for the patients could not afford to pay fees nearly covering their keep, let alone staff wages.

Sister Munroe was one of those to whom Florence Nightingale passed the Lamp. She had gained certificates in general and midwifery nursing, and in dispensing, in Melbourne. Then she had come to the West and taken sole charge of a government hospital at Wiluna on the isolated peak of the goldfields hundreds of miles from anywhere. Leaving in 1915 to join the A.I.F., she had been in France with the spearhead following retreating Germans and her account of the enemy's vacated hospitals were tragic beyond words. Not so her stories of Wiluna, especially those concerning the Aborigines, so human, droll, brave and intelligent, with whom she made friends.

But about Jack. Although the doctor was satisfied with his condition I was not. Sister told me he had asked for me when she questioned him concerning his next of kin. 'Send for Sally,' he'd said, 'if you want anyone. She's got some sense and she's a nurse. Never married, lives at Darlington, same name as me—called Mollie by most people.'

If Jack had read *The Boy in the Bush* he wouldn't have given me credit for much 'sense' I am sure, but there was a strong tie of blood between us—such as Lawrence had for his sisters. Best of all his relatives, however, he loved Nazeli's girl Judy and she him. I was dismayed, therefore, when he pointed to the window and began waving happily. 'Look, Sally,' he said, 'there's Judy off to school. I watch out for her every day.' Such visions often forebode death and when he asked why Dad and Mum hung around outside and didn't come in, I was scared. Then he began to speak of his mate on a 'show' with him at Bullfinch—twenty miles out—and showed me a test tube half full of pure gold specks they had taken from the little mine. 'See?' he said. 'We'll be rich yet, Sally. I want to leave all I have to Mittie to compensate her for taking care of me when I was so crook after the war—that bullet still in my jaw—I looked and behaved like a clown. I've made a will.'

As Sister was out he asked me to wash his feet. I washed them, though they were perfectly clean, and was frightened again in spite of the doctor's assurance.

He died that night.

As I sent a telegram to Mittie, another was handed to me. Judy had died at the same hour in Perth.

I was so dazed that the local R.S.L. took over, leaving me to do no more than choose a coffin. I found the carpenter in his office and realised from the black coat, white dicky, gloves and celluloid collar that he must also be the undertaker. 'You Jack's sister?' he asked. 'Well, I'll show you the coffin I done for meself. Jack can have it if you like. He was my corp at Gallipoli. A real sport he was. Never gave in, Jack didn't, leading us on, wounded as he was, till he fell.'

He showed me his masterpiece, decorated with elaborate carvings of hearts and doves and texts. Strangling my sobs I told him I thought it was beautiful and he asked me what he should put on the plate.

'Courage never dies,' I said, not knowing where the words came from.

'Them words suits Jack,' he said. 'He shall have the glass hearse too if I can borrow the baker's black 'oss to pull it. He's a Special, Jack is.'

'Come and look at him,' said Sister when I got back. 'There's no need to cry any more. Your brother will never grow old.'

'I don't want to see him,' I gasped.

'But he looks like a knight at rest after finding the Grail.'

So I had to go in to please her.

And now there thou liest, Sir Lancelot, I thought as I looked at him.

But it wasn't Sir Lancelot who came to the burial with us, but Jack my brother who had scorned ill luck with a quip and a jest and who seemed amused when the coffin proved too long for the grave. On the goldfields, you see, down-and-out prospectors eagerly take on digging graves in advance for a small sum, for although the ground is so hard they stand a chance of unearthing a 'slug' or perhaps even a seam of gold.

A mate then jerked his thumb towards the gate, and I remembered Jack had arranged for Mac the mailman to take me to Bullfinch that day to see his 'show' and 'cubby' and meet his cobber Jim. Mac was waiting so off I went.

Soon the sunshine and unfolding beauty of the land brought peace to my soul, and Mac, as he chatted, interest to my mind.

'Me dad,' he said, 'pushed a wheelbarrow here in the rush before the railway. Ma came with him, leading the goat. Dad swore because he had to wheel the barrow with provisions and water, and he didn't want to come. He was hefty, though a little weak in the crumpet, and Ma knew it. When they reached the Cross, the goat had a kid and Ma made him stay put. She sold the milk for a bob a mug and then they found water and she sent Dad to the shows around with buckets of it at half a dollar. Then a man in a cart of merchandise lost his horse and Ma made Dad buy him out and open a store. So when I come along they was all set, the railway running, and by and by the water pipe passing the door. Ma sent me to school in Fremantle to stay with her folk and be educated. Then I learnt about motor cars till I went to sea as purser's steward, and on to the war. Now I'm settled right here with wife and kids.'

We had passed out of the township with its hotel, butcher's, baker's, store and railway station, and on over the hard yellow ground into virgin bush. Gum trees of all sorts and sizes, interlarded with scrub, flourished triumphantly in spite of low rainfall and fierce summer sun. Here and there Mac pointed to pink pools of salt water that were claypans for most of the year. 'Camels carry water to Bullfinch,' he said, 'but there's a railway supposed to go out there soon.'

The rough rutty track did not worry Mac and when I settled down to bumping along, the beauty of the virgin land gat hold of me. The colouring was enchanting, the air clear as crystal and smelling like honey. Flocks of parrots flew overhead screeching with joy, having found nuts and seeds to feed on.

'But this isn't goldfield country!' I exclaimed.

'It's part of the Yilgarn all right,' said Mac. 'Prospectors came first, followed by the diggers to open it up. They spread around the better known fields and then the stockmen came in.' He waved his hand towards a few head of cattle peering through the scrub. 'Then come the farmers to clear and plough and seed the likely areas. We had such a grand crop of wheat cut round the Cross last season, you wouldn't believe.'

'I reckon,' he went on, 'right down to the south-west corner'll be wheatgrowing and farming land before long. Not north or east— that's the devil's, or the squatters', own with a chain of salt lakes twisting like a serpent round bloody rocks enough to scare the wits outa man and beast. Beyond them to the north lies the Murchison.'

'It's a long way from Buckingham Palace,' I mused, taking a deep breath of the golden air, and he fell silent till we reached Bullfinch.

This centre was named after a mine with an enormous iron wheel carrying trucks from a hole in the ground. The trucks turned, emptied of mullock and swung back into place on the moving wheel. Corrugated iron sheds and a camp or two were scattered around, and the rest of the town appeared to consist of a verandahless hotel. Here we had lunch—salt beef and beer. Then Jack's cobber, nervously twisting his old felt hat, took me to see the 'possie'.

Though a fine type with a long lean face, he looked furtive and did not speak at all. He led me to a shack within a pocket handker-chief enclosure where a tiny garden was laid out surrounded by upturned bottles buried half way in the red ground. Outside the door of the shack stood a ten-gallon tank and a Coolgardie hessian cooler. Within was a home-made table, the supports set in the mud floor, a stone fireplace, a stretcher on either side, with shelved packing cases for lockers.

So this was Jack's home! What more could a man want after all, I comforted myself, and then began to cry. Turning away, I found that the cobber was crying too. Sobs shook his frame and sheltering his wet eyes in the crook of his elbow he opened the gate for me and followed me to the car.

That's the last I saw of the cobber and whether there was a show or not we never knew. In fact Jack left nothing and his unlucky demon continued to grimace at me for some time. He had reared a foal and the lovely creature had been entered to race by a trainer. But the trainer had not been paid and we had to pass the filly over to him. Jack's banking account was a little overdrawn; his allotment— only a few shillings a week after all—was spent. That left only the two little cottages which were already mortgaged to Mittie. Then the Repatriation Department sent me a bill for the funeral.

Never have I been so angry. Nothing was going to make me use the money for *The Boy in the Bush* to pay this unjust debt. Jack had given the best of his youth fighting for his country and had returned from the war shattered and prematurely aged.

The spirit of generations of soldiers rose in me and since the R.S.L. could not aid me, I tackled the Repatriation Department which slammed the door in my face. So then I tried the quill. The telephone started ringing. First it was the newspaper: 'We have shown your letter to the Repat officials. They ask us to hold it.' Then the Department: 'We beg you to withdraw your letter to the newspaper.' 'No,' I said, 'not unless you withdraw that bill you have sent me for my brother's funeral. I have a doctor's statement to the effect that he died of thrombosis as a result of a war wound.' Half an hour later, the Department rang again: 'We have decided to meet half the account.' I replied: 'Then I'll ask the paper to publish half the letter.'

That did it. The account was settled by them and the letter withdrawn.

The letter Lawrence wrote to me about Jack's passing healed my wounded spirit and gave me new heart for endeavour.

Del Monte Ranch
Questa
New Mexico
28 August 1925

Dear Mollie Skinner,

I sent you a letter yesterday, & last night came yours telling that your brother was dead. He had no luck: one could see in his face, that he never would have luck. Perhaps it's really true, lucky in money, unlucky in love. But as a matter of fact, I believe he really never *wanted* to make good. At the bottom of his soul, he preferred to drift penniless through the world. I think if I had to choose, myself, between being a Duke of Portland, or having a million sterling & forced to live up to it, I'd rather, far, far rather be a penniless tramp. There is deep inside one a revolt against the fixed thing, fixed society, fixed money, fixed homes, even fixed love. I believe that was what ailed your brother: he couldn't bear the social fixture of everything. It's what ails me too.

And after all, he lived his life & had his mates wherever he went. What more does a man want? So many old bourgeois people live on and on, and *can't* die, because they have never been in life at all. Death's not sad, when one has lived.

And that again is what I think about writing a novel: one can live so intensely with one's characters and the experience one creates or records, it is a life in itself, far better than the vulgar thing people call life, jazzing and motoring & so on. No, every day I live I feel more disgust at the thing these Americans call life. Ten times better die penniless on a goldfield.

But be sure of my sympathy.

D. H. Lawrence

24

Chirp! Chirp!

The other letter that Lawrence had written came by another route.

Del Monte Ranch
Questa
New Mexico
28 Aug. 1925

Dear Mollie Skinner,

I am glad you are safe with Miss Beakbane at "Leithdale"—you will have enough things to do, and sunshine & space, and time to write. I wish I could be at Leithdale myself, for a few months. My wife loved it there, so did I.

The summer has gone by here so quickly. I am quite well again, in the mountains with my horses, & the cow Susan. We are leaving for New York on Sept 10th. I am sorry to go. Yet it's good, not to stay too much alone, & not to be too long in America. This is a heavy, stubborn sort of continent, without much elan, no natural joy.—I suppose we shall be in England for the month of October, then go south, to the Mediterranean. I have been waiting all summer for *Black Swans*. What is Cape doing? I'll look him up when I get to London, and see. And if the book is out, I'll get it & review it for one of the monthlies, if I can. I'll have a try, when I'm in London.

Over here, things aren't very good. Seltzer is nearly bankrupt, and only pays me small doles, out of all he owes me. I've had nothing for *Boy in the Bush*, at all. But I suppose it will come. Anyhow I'll see they send you a few dollars, when any are squeezed out of Seltzer. We have no luck.

How's your new novel going?—Mine is being held over to Spring 1926. It's called *The Plumed Serpent*: it's the Mexican book. I'm glad it's not coming immediately. I get so weary of the public, it's smallness & fatuity.

I wonder if there's anything you'd like particularly to read? If there is, tell me, and I'll send it you from London. C/O Curtis Brown always finds me there: 6 Henrietta St. W.C.2.
I shall look for word from you in London. Never bother about publishers & public; one goes one's own way, bit by bit.

My wife sends her regards.

Yrs
D. H. Lawrence

It was October when these letters arrived, so our summer had almost begun. There was a lot to do, for Leithdale had gone down through 'letting' and we had to find a new staff. Our tenants had sent Martin to the Old Men's Home but we got through a registry office two 'assisted immigrants'—very réchercé—and a staunch little local maid to help in the kitchen. Her name was Annie Samuel, the man's Lardie (you couldn't help adding 'da' under your breath). He waxed his moustache and had a wife who had opened a hat shop in Perth, but Annie proved a treasure, able and willing to do anything in a well-run house, and very pleasant.

Everything was now on a different footing and Mittie went off to join Estelle in the East. We never saw either of them again for they both died over there.

Though I was still craving to write the goldfields novel, constant interruptions prevented my getting on with it. But I managed a short story, 'The Hand', about a goldfields hospital, and sent it to the *Adelphi*, edited in London by Middleton Murry, and wrote some of Sister Munroe's yarns about the Wiluna Aborigines which were published in *The West Australian* under the title 'Men Are We'.

Lawrence's letters became as the strains of a distant violin drowned by the rat-a-tat-tat of drums and bugles ringing in my ears. They drowned the Voice too and loosened the pressure of the Hand. I marched along like a puffed up little boy singing 'Pack up your troubles in your old kit bag and smile, smile, smile', for publishers and public had come up to expectations. Volumes of *Black Swans* had arrived in Perth stamped with Cape's distinctive mark, and showers of press cuttings came by every mail from London. The *Times Literary Supplement* gave the book a column, the *Daily News* three-quarters, the *Daily Telegraph* half, the *Observer* and *John*

o'London less space, and less criticism, *Punch*, the *Sketch* and even
the *New Statesman* more praise. Other papers followed suit from all
over the place including the Colonies. Australia took little notice of
it, though some of my friends made a fuss of me.

A cousin gave me a reception at the Karrakatta Club and my name
was returned to the visitors' list at Government House. But 'What a
pity,' they said, 'that Mollie let the notorious D. H. Lawrence spoil
her first book.' Perhaps they looked on me as a future Marie Corelli,
who was very popular in those days.

Such comments of course belonged to a different world from that
of Katharine Susannah Prichard whose friendship has lasted all my
life since; and Henrietta Drake-Brockman who in her youth studied
art before she took to writing books. Mary and Elizabeth Durack, who
were still children though already steeped in art and literature,
Ernestine Hill and John K. Ewers and his wife Jean I did not meet
till later. All these people are my treasured friends today.

Just for a moment let us consider how the vast empty State was
pressing down on the centres not yet called cities. The lovely university at Crawley had not been built and culture was still more or less
asleep. But it is always inherent in the heart of a growing nation,
and those who knew its intestimable value were striving for it. Thus,
while fine new men took over in the medical profession, business
concerns grew, the Technical School introduced cultural classes, and
Labor and Liberal politics strove to uplift the swaying State, we
carried on. Women gained power. Edith Cowan took her seat as
the first lady member of parliament in the Commonwealth; a few
women doctors achieved practices; artists formed groups; and Emily
Pelloe published her beautifully illustrated book about our amazing
wildflowers. She and others started a Women Writers' Club on which
committee I remained until it melted into the W.A. Branch of the
Fellowship of Australian Writers.

Western Australia was a wide, empty and still largely unknown
State, far, far away from European centres of culture, but it was
mine; I was born of its travail and loved it. If only I could write
about it and its people! But it was not to be. I had to earn my living.

Still I was a happy bird and life went on without passion and
without pain. Nellie Beakbane I loved as did everyone and in most
things we managed to meet each other half way. She did not like
it much when I bought a hundred chicks to rear on my own account,

but presently she nobly compromised by purchasing an expensive set of surgical instruments to caponise them! It was a proper mess-up. I was far too blind to help caponise cockerels, and too inexpert to hold them still for Nellie.

After that I handed over my pets to Lardie, and helped her to re-cover the lounge suite. Cutting and contriving to make expensive material fit where it won't is far from being my cup of tea, but I did my best.

As the hot weather came on and our guests decreased to the few who preferred the hills air to the beaches, the indoor expenses decreased, but the outdoor costs rose. Lardie, when approached with an inflated produce merchant's bill, said the horse, cows and poultry were eating the same as usual but that my growing chicks were insatiable. No use saying they didn't eat hay or corn, so, the covers now finished, I took them over again, running them in the wire-netted orchard and feeding them on scraps and a little wheat.

Then, as the chicks grew big and strong, such a cackle and a crowing came every morning from the orchard that we sent to the markets for crates to send them away. This meant all hands climbing the trees at sundown to catch the infuriated birds that were then shoved, pecking and cackling, into the crates. The little maid enjoyed it thoroughly—but Lardie gave notice. Nellie solaced him by saying rearing poultry wasn't worth the bother and we would use what were left for the table. So he stayed.

No one yet knew which were cockerels and which pullets, so the valuable pullets graced the table and the cockerels did not cease to crow.

By now I had sufficient money from *The Boy in the Bush*—which sum Nellie Beakbane would not touch—to buy a car, and as provision merchants' bills were still consuming our profits I suggested we got rid of the cows and horse, bought our milk and used my car to carry it.

Nellie rejected this suggestion. She liked to have a presentable man about the place, she said, and pointed out that the old horse dragging the ancient phaeton up the hill, and unlimited milk and cream, were part of Leithdale's attraction. Actually, as I later discovered, she thought I would be quite incapable of driving a car.

Summer descended with a vengeance and a three day heat wave led to bushfires. One of these roaring through the empty ranges from the east in the arms of a mighty wind came sweeping down on us, blazing over hills and valleys as far as the eye could see. Though the Mundaring Weir pipeline to Kalgoorlie was only a few miles away, Darlington had no water laid on at that time, but volunteer fire fighters came from all directions to help beat the inferno back with wet sacks and green branches; to cut breaks or set other fires alight to meet the oncoming blast.

We watched with fascinated horror the great circle of glowing ash left behind on the hilltops, while the main fire leaped onward, consuming everything in its hungry path. Knowing that after winter rains the charred trees would sprout new foliage and wildflowers bloom again, we were none the less terrified as whirling winds carried grass flares to start new fires.

When Nellie caught sight of Lardie standing petrified with his back against a wall, she thrust into his hands a huge billy of tea and pushed him with it towards the firefighters. It was a courageous act, for she was sick with fear of bushfires. Generally the morale was good. The helpless guests changed for dinner as usual. The little maid went on preparing the meal, the lady-help setting the tables, while I hopped around whistling.

After dinner Nellie was discovered out to it, on the lounge in the hall, being fanned by a blackened firefighter.

'O.K.,' he said, 'sea breeze is up driving the flames back on themselves. She's a real sport, bringing tea, we was about done in and she kept bailing it out to us till she collapsed.'

That was the end of Lardie who, while the fighters paused to drink their tea, had been pressed into action with a wet sack. His moustache singed, his collar and tie dangling round his neck, his trousers scorched, the soles of his boots burnt, his hands blistered, he took himself off.

Annie's young brother took his place and everyone was happy and full of laughter and lightheardedness—including Nellie. This may have been because of a windfall from the shares which she liked to dabble in, and because a splendid retired contractor named Shepherd undertook to give advice on alterations and repairs to Leithdale.

Nellie at last gave in about my buying a car and I learnt to drive and bought a Baby Austin. Police traffic laws did not include eye tests at that time and perhaps they are not so very important after all, for filmed eyes give a person a sort of ultra ray called a sixth sense— a warning of danger and ability to avoid it. Besides this, fingers, even toes, seem to see, and voices, laughter, sighs, breathing and footsteps convey meaning. I drove thousands of miles during the next fifteen years without a blot on my licence.

Nellie refused to get in the car if I was at the wheel but she met me half way by taking an interest in its works. She even arranged for us both to take a course in mechanics at the Technical School, but this left me stone cold. She kept the toy in order.

By that time I had wakened to the fact that my will had become Nellie's. And that the way I was settling into a groove was minus endeavour, minus worth, minus everything I longed for in my inmost soul.

Then came this letter from Lawrence:

Villa Bernada
Spotorno
10 April, 1926

Dear Molly Skinner,

I have been putting off writing to you because I was sad about 'Black Swans'. It was too much of a cinema piece and stayed on the surface, and I wanted so much to like it and then really I didn't.

We have been here for some months, and now next week are moving on. I am awfully glad to be back in Italy. It seems so easy and it gives one a good deal.

What is 'Men are We' about? I do hope you will make it as real as you can, and not let it fly off into too much dramatics. Murry showed me your little sketch about the Hospital and I thought it was good; but you ought to hold yourself in and discipline yourself as you write.

If I can help you with anything be sure to let me know. Write me c/o Curtis Brown. I should have written long ago except for feeling sad about 'Black Swans'. One day we shall surely see you again, either in Australia or Europe. As soon as my play is out I shall send you a copy.

Yours ever,
D. H. Lawrence

That letter made me sit up. He didn't like *Black Swans*, but he did like 'The Hand'. He thought I could write if I held myself in, and he was still willing to help me.

25

Fulfilment

It was May again and I walked up the hill into the bush that had been scoured by the fire. Blackened scrub whipped dark streaks on my clothes; the hollow trunks of trees that had not resisted the burning looked grim and desolate. But lo, the frail green shoots of grass, fern and herbage gleamed golden in the sunshine, and in the shadows softly silver. It was a lovely day after rain, the unscathed trees spreading their everlasting leaves against the pale blue sky and casting their hard brown nuts merrily at intervals upon the ground. Some of the banksias stood erect, with blackened seed-cones and scorched leaves, while others, unharmed, flaunted triumphant blossoms. Here and there lay patches of flowering scrub, their blooms primrose yellow or lily white, and from the burnt carpet of the flattened bush shot flower spikes of purple hovea.

The June, July and August rains would bring more and brighter blossoms and lovely delicate flowers, and the rosellas, chortling 'Twenty-eight, twenty-eight' would swing, pecking, from the branches of the trees. How was it Lawrence missed these birds that flashed with rainbow brilliance through the bush?

Well, he didn't notice everything, I thought; I shall just have to show him something more about our Golden West. If only I were not surrounded by obligations! And then, out there in the ageless bush the Voice spoke. *Obligations, nothing! You know very well you are clinging to them to escape Endeavour. You enjoy living at ease in a fine house in the loving care of another and going to Perth as Someone of Quality whose paltry book has achieved some sort of success. You are growing soft and silly within, and hard and selfish without. What do you think God gave you afflictions for? Surely for something better than this?*

But, I found myself storming, what the hell *was* His heavenly

166

purpose? I could, I knew, help mothers bring their babies into the world but I was far from sure I could deliver a satisfactory book to Curtis Brown. Writing was, besides, a terrible effort and perhaps it was, as Nellie said about rearing chicks, 'not worth the bother'.

Then I looked down at a spear of hovea thrusting its head through the charred ground, and I was ashamed.

Going back into the everyday I felt the Hand again on my shoulder, the Voice checking impatience, wilfulness, criticism of others—my greatest sin—pride, and all the other mean little sins that Christ made manifest and are harder for man to forgive of man than the greater ones. Not that we seemed to have much to forgive each other that happy-go-lucky season at Leithdale. We were very busy in hectic rushes and as some monk wrote long ago, work is a form of worship in itself.

When things quietened down Mr Shepherd arrived with his lad, cart and horse, ladders and boxes of tools, and discussions about the alterations began. These were beyond my pocket and desires, so I begged to be allowed to pay another helper's wages—if one was needed—and take a job as relieving matron where my true skill was needed. Nellie did not make any how-d'you-do about it, being vastly preoccupied with Mr Shepherd's advice. A giant fig tree must be removed—it was unsettling the foundations—the huge corrugated iron building at the back could come down and be converted into a new kitchen, the whole interior colour-washed . . .

This all seems far apart from Lawrence. But is it? It was the flow of the river of life; the deep-seated flow of blood, and sparkling overflow of companionship and friendships, the restless currents of loss and new contacts—the Now we all live in when a month can be so interminably long and a year so appallingly short.

Every mortal seeks love and appreciation. The urge is universal and we know that when unhappily frustrated or over-stressed, it leads to perversion and crime. It can lead to great spiritual combat, heart-break and tears but these can also lead to sunshine and development —in other words, to God.

I did not know how Lawrence fared from the day I received the foregoing letter. I had no idea that vicious attacks of tuberculosis were now consuming him, or how he was fighting on, defying the invidious public and writing his ultimato, *Lady Chatterley's Lover*, to throw into the arena like an exploding bomb. Nor did I know that he had taken to painting pictures that would be called obscene. Of his drawings I knew only one, and that was the jacket on the American edition of *The Boy in the Bush*. It was enchanting in its way—though hardly Australian. Blue on white, it depicted a huge kangaroo inquisitively looking round the bole of a palm against which leant an exhausted boy, his torso bare, his legs in breeches and striped stockings, and thrown aside, not an old felt hat—but a sombrero.

In fact I knew little more at the time of Lawrence's pilgrimage through life than what I had learned through contact with him in Australia and from his letters.

Two years passed before another letter came and that was the last. To explain it: After living as it were in the third dimension of this strange, still almost unknown country north of the south-west, I finished *Eve in the Land of Nod*, and not in the least knowing that Lawrence was strained almost beyond endurance, physically by consuming illness and mentally by vitriolic criticism, sent it to him, asking if he cared to take it on as he had *The Boy*. I confessed he was right about *Black Swans*. It was a failure too, commercially, though Edward Garnett had said it was so damned damned good as well as so damned damned bad, and though the critics had called it 'a book of unusual quality' and said 'Here is Empire in the making, swift movement, reality and romance' . . .

I don't remember eagerly waiting for Lawrence's answer, for having established myself at last as a white-capped scrub wren I was quite happy nursing as a district midwife. I only remember, after it came, thinking, 'That's that. I'll give it up and concentrate on nursing—it pays better, and gives me much greater satisfaction. Besides, I'm a good midwife and that brings the love of mothers, and a tenderness in myself for little babies. After all what is more wonderful, or important to a nation, than new life and the fulfilling of a purpose in helping it grow healthy and strong?

Here is the letter:

Hotel Beau Rivage
Bandol
France
3 Decem. 1928

Dear Molly Skinner
Your Ms. came on here, and I have read it all, and am returning it to you. I can't do with it as I did with Boy in the Bush—

that was a tour de force which one can do once, but not twice. And you see I know nothing of gold-camps, never saw a black boy except in the streets of Sydney, and know nothing of medicine. How can I re-create an atmosphere of which I know nothing? I should only make silly howlers. I suspect you of making a few. A mine, for example, would, I feel sure, be much more difficult to fake.—And then I really don't like your Jim men—who appeal to women by their exquisite pathos. Exquisite pathos puts me dead off men.—Still, the book has good points, and in a way is the most developed of your efforts. If I were to suggest anything, I should suggest that it's form might be the form of a sort of diary—use the *I* again—and write in little sections, no chapters, just those little flashes of scenes and incidents, made briefer and more poignant, following one another with the hap-hazard of event. If you set about it, you could do two or three little sections a week, and make each brief, poignant telling. Cut out what you don't want—the man dying in the buggy, at the very beginning, for example, it has no point. Make it all a little more inward and personal. Don't make your Nurse Leigh quite so sprightly—make her loneliness a bit more poignant. Put in more of the ugliness— and the pain of the ugliness—more of the rather repulsive quality of people of that camp sort. Don't be so swimmily sympathetic and rather school-teacherishly good. And you might make a real book of it, much better than Black Swans. Buy a nice exercise book, and do it fragment by fragment, as an intimate experience.

There, you won't thank me for all this unasked-for advice which you get in place of more strenuous help. But I'm sorry to see you disappointed. I'm sorry I can't really do what you wish.—Remember us both to Miss Beakbane, and all our good wishes to you.

D. H. Lawrence

A little over a year later I heard Lawrence was dead, and reading those last poems I knew he had revealed something of the beauty of creation and of the Creator to the world at large.

And if as weeks go round, in the dark of the moon
My spirit darkens and goes out, and soft strange gloom
pervades my movements and my thoughts and words,
Then I shall know that I am walking still
With God, we are close together now the moon's in shadow . . .

And if, in the changing phases of man's life,
I fall in sickness and in misery,
My wrists seem broken and my heart seems dead,
And strength is gone and my life is only the leavings of a life;
And still among it all, snatches of lovely oblivion and snatches
    of renewal,
Odd wintry flowers upon the withered stem, yet new strange
    flowers,
Such as my life has not brought forth before, new blossoms
    of me:
Then I must know that still
I am in the hands of the unknown God:
He is breaking me down to his own oblivion,
To send me forth on a new morning, a new man.

APPENDIX
Published Works of M. L. Skinner

Midwifery Made Easy (1913)

Letters of a V.A.D. (*nom de plume* R. E. Leake; London: Andrew Melrose, 1918)

The Boy in the Bush (with D. H. Lawrence, London: Martin Secker, August 1924. New York: Thomas Seltzer, 1924)

Black Swans (London: Jonathan Cape, 1925)

Men are We, Aboriginal stories (Perth: People's Publishing Co., 1927)

Tucker Sees India (London: Secker and Warburg, 1937)

W.X.—Corporal Smith (Perth: R. S. Sampson, 1941)

When Skies are Blue (Introduction by J. K. Ewers. Perth: Imperial Printing Co., 1946)

The Witch of Welleway (*The Bulletin*, Sydney, 22 February 1956)

See also: *D. H. Lawrence and M. L. Skinner* (with G. E. Mayman, *Australian Observer*, Melbourne, 24 July 1948)